The Next Level: SUPERCHARGED

The Next Level: Supercharged
By Dr. Rob Garcia, Ed.D

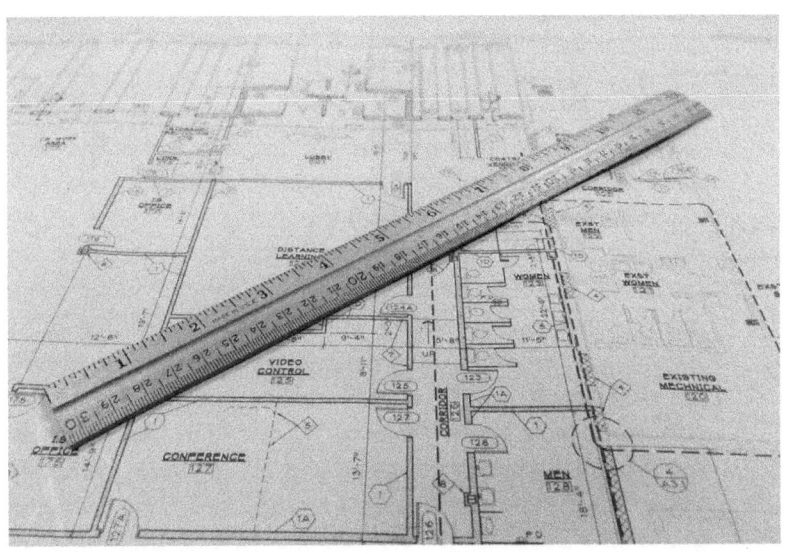

Copyright © 2016 by Dr. Rob Garcia and Blue Dragon Publishing

The Next Level: SUPERCHARGED

Testimonials about Dr. Rob Garcia

"Rob Garcia has absolute confidence and belief in himself. He accepts his past, owns responsibility for the present and prepares for change in the future. We all possess within us what it takes to be happy, content, and successful, and Rob is proof of that." - Jana C.

"Your friendship, loyalty, drive and unparalleled ambition has inspired me to not only set my own goals, but also has given me the courage to accomplish and reach them-- you are a "closer" Rob, through our friendship and these many years, I am a better man from knowing you." - Jeff C

"Dr. Garcia is a great friend, mentor, teacher, and amongst other things a motivator. Before I met Dr. Garcia I was a good student travelling through a rough road in life. My grades had spiraled out of control, my teachers had lost faith in me academically and I had found myself in a hole I felt I couldn't get out of. It wasn't until I met a young Garcia, who would see beyond an academic performance that would begin our friendship and it was through Garcia I had learned how to channel my focus and energy into achieving goals. By relating with me and telling his story, I found motivation and I saw possibility. Without his advice, guidance, or friendship, I can honestly say I don't know if I would have reached the next level of my life." - Lou Cortes

The Next Level: SUPERCHARGED

"I have known Rob for about 6 years now. In that time he has done a lot in my life to motivate me, make me a better person, helped me through rough times and much more. Most recently I admitted a failure to him. See, I am in the Air Force also, and physical fitness is a requirement for us all, and it is my biggest weakness in my daily life. Over the last year I became very lazy in that area, and with my fit test looming I reached out for help.

Anytime I have an issue that I can't figure out myself, my go to is Rob, as he has been an amazing mentor and life coach to me for a long time. I told him how I had grown lazy, and I had nobody to blame but myself. He set me straight. He sent me a Skinny Dragon plan that got me on the road to getting back in shape. He gave me diet ides of what and how much to eat. At the time I spoke to him, my run was 16 minutes long, and I could do 20 or less push up/sit ups. My waist was a ridiculous 42.

This is an automatic failure for the Air Force. I did my best to follow his advice and it paid off. Earlier this week I contacted him and gave him an update. I was able to pass my practice tests, but just barely with a score of 76, 75 is a passing score. I still needed an extra push especially for my waist, and he was quick to pass the information. He told me cold showers, more running, no flour no sugar. I had no choice but to follow as my test was just days away. I took that test today and passed with a score of 81.6.

Since talking to Rob about this issue, I shaved 3 minutes 10 seconds off my run time, I added 30+ to my push up and sit ups, and shrunk my waist from a 42 to a 37.5. Here is the best thing about having Rob as a mentor, he will never tell you what you want to hear, but will always tell you what you need to hear, and most of the time, it sucks. Never once though has his mentorship and advice lead me down the wrong path. I am thankful for him and how quick he is to help someone above himself." - Ken M, Fl

The Next Level: SUPERCHARGED

Also by Dr. Rob Garcia:

Aiming Higher

Teen Juggernaut

The 2014 San Diego Technical Careers Guide

The Skinny Dragon Diet

Utopia

All books available on the Blue Dragon Website at www.bluedragonent.com

The Next Level: SUPERCHARGED

This book is dedicated to anyone that ever dared to fight the hand that life dealt them- Dr. Rob Garcia

The Next Level: SUPERCHARGED

The Next Level: SUPERCHARGED

Table of Contents

Chapter 1: Introduction 9
Chapter 2: Next Level Concepts 13
Chapter 3: History of Self Education 21
Chapter 4: The GMOSC Model 27
Chapter 5: Research 33
Chapter 6: Emulation 39
Chapter 7: Tutelage 45
Chapter 8: Life Experience 51
Chapter 9: Formal Education 55
Chapter 10: Repetitive Practice 61
Chapter 11: Creation 65
Chapter 12: Socratic Method 69
Chapter 13: Immersion 73
Chapter 14: Emotional Investment 77
Chapter 15: Masterminds/Groups 83
Chapter 16: HLSME 87
Chapter 17: Diagramming 91
Chapter 18: Neutropic Drugs 97
Chapter 19: Trifecta 101
Chapter 20: Reverse Engineering 104
Chapter 21: Next Step: Hollywood 109
Chapter 22: GMOSC In Action 113
Chapter 23: Real Life Examples 119
Team Hoyt
Katrina Lucero
Frankie Hill
Joseph Kapacziewski
Josh and Jill Stanton
Chapter 18: Epilogue 150

The Next Level: SUPERCHARGED

The Next Level: SUPERCHARGED

Chapter 1: Introduction

The Next Level: SUPERCHARGED

Welcome to The Next Level: Supercharged. This book will be about rapid skill or career building. Ever wondered how some people can start a new job or a hobby and in a month they are *really* good at it? I am always reminded of the Matrix where Neo jacks into the mainframe and can download skills that would take years to learn on his own.

While this book won't be as fast as the Matrix (sorry kung fu practitioners, you still have to learn your forms and strikes the old fashioned way), you can be assured that I have found some very helpful ways to cut down on your learning curve.

Imagine the ability to choose a skill or career you are interested in, and learning the best techniques to improve at it. It could be something as simple as photographing birds to something technical, such as designing and building your own electronic devices. You read this book, identify where you currently stand, in regards to talent, retention and skill, and learn 15 ways to get even better at it!

I have been fascinated with intelligence for about a decade now. A decidedly late bloomer, I had many academic difficulties as a young man, and failed out of high school once, and college twice. It just seemed like I looked at things differently, and in many cases, was teased about it, sometimes rather viciously. In hindsight, I had a very challenging childhood and was never given the opportunity or motivation to push myself.

In my early 20's, I started to seek and develop knowledge rapidly. I inadvertently was hired as a high school teacher in Engineering, which required me to learn trigonometry, algebra, pre calculus, technical documentation, and a computer program called Inventor………….in five days. Keep in mind, I had never been an engineer, never attained an engineering degree, nor could tell you what they even did. I can assure you, my learning curve was *steep*. The first two years were rough. My fifth and final year of

The Next Level: SUPERCHARGED

teaching, I had a letter from the Secretary of Education on my wall for a 25 page proposal I had written for the creation of the ideal high school, had been nominated for Teacher of the Year, and was running an Academy of Engineering.

How did I go from one extreme to another? By using several of the concepts outlined in a book I would write nearly ten years later. At the time, I had no idea that these ideas would help me to become a better professional. In several instances of my life, I have used techniques to improve in several aspects of my life. Sometimes with amazing results.

The Next Level is an exciting concept in Intelligence Development. I wanted to write a book that could help *anyone*, from an intern wanting to work their way up in the company, to a truck driver wanting to be more efficient at their job.

This book is broken down into different components; the first few chapters outline the theory of the Next Level structure. I delve into a brief history of self-education, and then discuss your first method of self assessment, the GMOSC model. It's something I developed as a way for you to quickly figure out where you stand at any skill or talent.

Once you have located your level, I introduce a series of techniques that I have listed for your ascension to the Next Level. I discuss the advantages, disadvantages, a description of what each technique entails, and throw in a few examples of the most effective methods of adopting these techniques.

After you have read about these 10 techniques, I discuss higher intellect, as depicted in movies and books. I want you to be able to see it in action and learn from it. Popular media can be an outstanding teacher, as long as the source is tangible, and is based on attainable methods.

After you have learned about higher intellect and skill building in popular culture, you will be shown three fictional people and how they could potentially use this book

The Next Level: SUPERCHARGED

to accelerate their goals even though they have vastly different backgrounds and goals.

The last chapter contains real interviews with successful people that have used Next Level concepts to advance their lives.
With the techniques I have outlined within this book, I have no doubt that you will have what it takes to go to..........

2016 Update

What you are reading is the upgraded version of the Next Level. I wrote this book around 2013 with the hope that the concepts would take off and people would be speed learning like crazy. I received some pretty good feedback but felt like I had grown a lot in 3 years.

This book was one of my "hidden gems." A book that has so much potential to change lives yet never took off. So I revisited it. I examined it and added many new features and design elements. This new revision has the following:
*A smaller, cleaner font

*An interview with Josh and Jill Stanton, CEOs of Screw the 9 to 5 Community

*SIX new learning techniques for mastering anything

*A redesigned format for the GMOSC

*5 in-book worksheets for helping you create your learning plan

*New content in each chapter

The Next Level: SUPERCHARGED

Chapter 2:
Next Level Contents

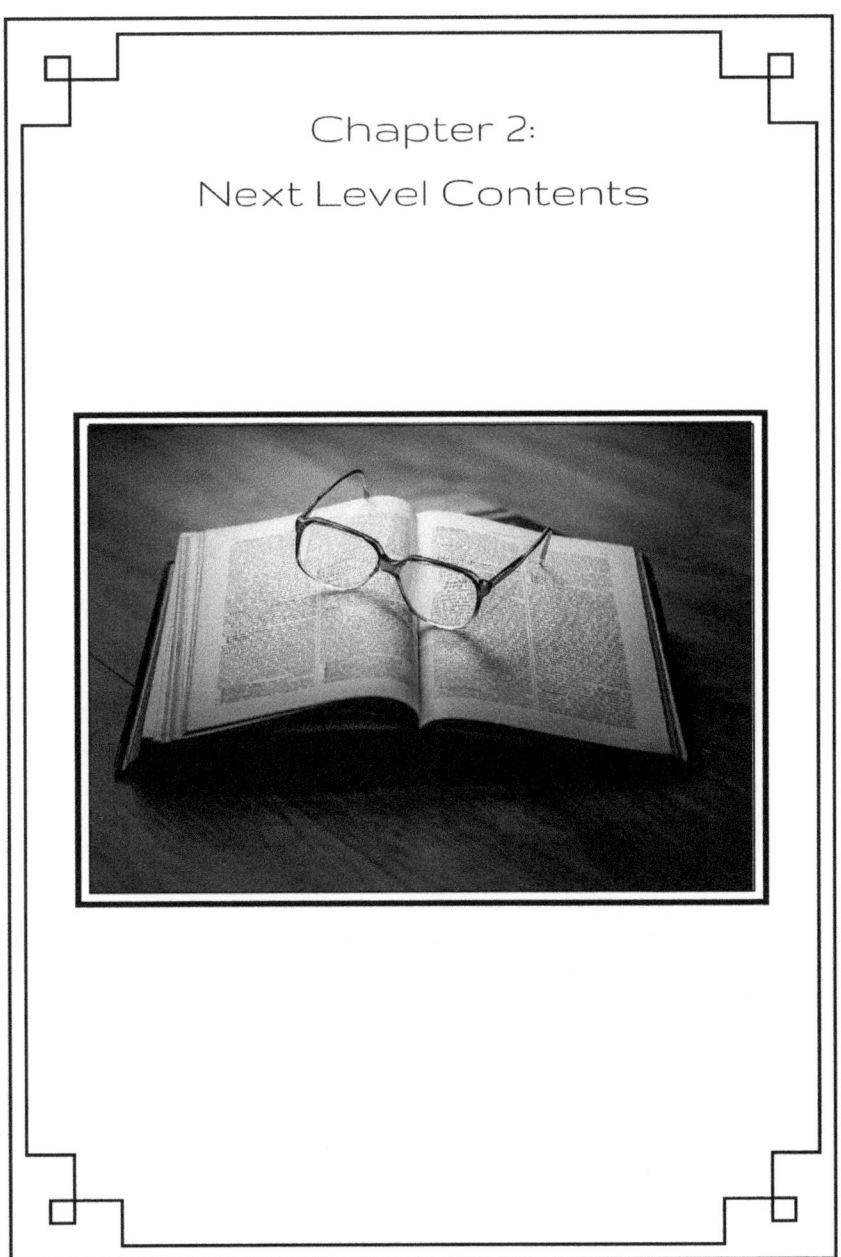

The Next Level: SUPERCHARGED

Believe it or not, nearly all these ideas were prevalent in my life and one day at work after a heroic amount of morning caffeine, it struck me: Why not write a book that brings together all of my experiences in teaching, the military, skill building, and self improvement? I had already written two books for teens, Aiming Higher, and Teen Juggernaut, so I had an idea of what it takes to develop a person and improve them. I looked at my life experiences:

*Interest in electronics; attended three schools for it

*Supervisor in Air Force B-52 maintenance squadron specializing in technical electronic navigation, avionic, landing, and radar devices

*High school engineering teacher specializing in mechanical and electrical engineering

*Doctoral degree specializing in Education with an emphasis on Project Based Learning.

So basically, you have a guy that grew up in a low income family, left home at 18, moved 1500 miles away, and after several failed attempts at attaining an education, joined the military and finished his education, learned to build up skills in subordinates, and ended up teaching a highly technical subject to minority students that in most cases had learning difficulties.

Trust me, writing a doctoral dissertation that is roughly 120 pages plus 6 years of classes, revisions, and residencies, teaches you to how to develop your knowledge on a topic. In my case, the topic was effective instruction to a series of learners with various levels of familiarity.

During my six year doctoral journey, I heavily studied Project Based Learning, which essentially is "learning by doing." I learned about how people throughout history gained skills, even when they didn't have access to formal education due to poverty, geographic isolation, or lack of desire to learn.

The Next Level: SUPERCHARGED

I started to compile a list of several great movies and tv shows that dealt with skill building and rapid acquisition of intelligence because some of us are visual learners. I then started to think about ranking systems and how they appear nearly everywhere in life.

Using my background as a military supervisor, I developed my own specialized ranking system, the GMOSC, so that you could self identify where you currently stand. Here are the main concepts behind The Next Level and a brief explanation:

Self Education

Self education is the act of learning about a subject or acquiring a skill *contingent upon your own devices*. That's just a fancy way of saying, "I taught myself how." There are several methods, but the common consensus is that you do not have formal instruction, a teacher, or a mentor.

Self education is always a very controversial topic because it is looked down upon by academics and formal institutions of higher learning. If you believe this is the best way to learn, you are in good company. Famous examples of self educated people of note include Edison, Lincoln, Simon Cowell, Sean Connery, Ben Franklin, and John D. Rockefeller. This list is not to denounce formal education, but rather to demonstrate that with the proper motivation and desire, a person can self educate to success.

Autodidactic learners have the potential to accomplish amazing things. They are devout consumers of knowledge and information and should not be treated any differently from "mainstream" learners.

The Next Level: SUPERCHARGED

> **Dr. Rob's Notes:**
> Famous autodidacts (self learners) are EVERYWHERE:
> *Frank Lloyd Wright Architect
> *David Bowie - Musician
> *Rodney Mullen - Pro Skateboarder
> *Henry Ford - Automaker
> *Michael Faraday - Scientist
> *Da Vinci - Inventor
> *Eminem - Rapper
> *Louis L'amour - Famous Western Author

Ranking/Hierarchal Structure

Ranking structures are *everywhere*. Think about your first day as a freshman in high school. Remember seeing the seniors and thinking, "*I can't wait to be like them one day.*"

Unconsciously, you were seeking your Next Level, although in a simplified form. Ranking structures are found in the workplace, the military, video games, martial arts, car races, sporting events, even the drive through line at McDonald's! Don't believe me? Do you want to be the last car in an 8 car line, or the car at the window, getting your food?

As a general rule, a higher ranking can potentially include the following:
- Better pay
- More demands upon time
- Elevated status
- Expectations of higher levels of performance
- Increased benefits/perks
- Higher level of responsibility
- More attention
- Greater scrutiny

The Next Level: SUPERCHARGED

- The privilege of leadership
- The burden of command

Notice how I worded that list? It was to demonstrate that while the Next Level is a natural desire for your advancement, you should have a good idea of what will be expected of you. The grass isn't always greener. A desire to advance should be equally coupled with a grasp of what the Next Level has in store for you.

Self Assessment

Self assessment came up numerous times in my doctoral studies of Project Based Learning. In its basic form, it means to reflect upon your performance or actions, and accurately capture in words how you think you did. Is a biased? Possibly. Is it important? Definitely. Using the GMOSC for your self assessment will help you to honestly and accurately place yourself.

Methods of Improvement

The "meat" of this fine book. I compiled a list of techniques from various sources that ranged to scientifically proven methods to Facebook friend suggestions (no, really, and some of them were GOOD). By reading about the various methods of skill improvement, you will be able to find the 1 or 10 that help you to grow at your chosen skill or field. In order to make the list, it had to have the following criteria:

*Proven and significant success by someone using it
*Easy to use
*Available to anyone
*Affordable, if not free
*Can be used by nearly anyone in nearly any field (from a 10th grader in San Jose to a 70 year old retiree in Florida)

The Next Level: SUPERCHARGED

Popular Culture as Education

I felt it was important to include this type of instruction for a few reasons. My personal opinion is that as a whole, television is responsible for a lot of intellectual regression. However, a person that spends a lot of time watching shows that are educational, or pertain to a specific area of interest, can benefit.

To effectively paraphrase one of my former students, "I just hate reading, it's so boring!" So for you visual learners, I have included a chapter just for you, so that you can seek out what The Next Level looks like, according to Hollywood and popular culture. No, there won't be a test but you'll probably see some great shows and movies.

Practical Applications

For this chapter, I invented three very different, fictional people. Although they are all made up in my imagination, they all are a product of experiences in my life. By showing you the various ways that they use the GMOSC and techniques shown, you can make a better choice for your own life/situation.

Real Life Examples

For this section, I found five amazing people that let me interview them. Every one of them accomplished some very amazing things against great odds. They shared their secrets and life philosophies with me.

Why Seek The Next Level?

Human beings are naturally adaptive and hierarchy-based. It is the very nature of human beings to question their own existence and want to improve their life situations. My

The Next Level: SUPERCHARGED

own personal crusade for improvement was brought upon by a childhood and upbringing that was defined by drugs, poverty, criminal behavior around me, lack of role models, and more misery than a child should ever know.

These events did not make me a victim, they made me a pioneer in my chosen field of mentorship and self improvement.

No matter what your status, education, or career, the fact that you are reading this book is indicative of your desire to better yourself. It is my utmost wish that the things you read bring you higher intellect, motivate you to be an EXPERT in your field, and push you to achieve more than you ever thought possible.

The Next Level: SUPERCHARGED

The Next Level: SUPERCHARGED

Chapter 3: My Own History of Self Education

The Next Level: SUPERCHARGED

The subject of self education has long been a controversial topic within the confines of formal academic structure. Looked down upon by many in the highest tiers of academia, this form of instruction is so important that I deemed it worthy of its own chapter. This topic is not presented to defame the benefits of a formal education, but to suggest that a symbiotic relationship can exist between the two.

Take for example the roles that education played in the military during World War II. The enlisted man typically was barely graduated from high school and his unit was commanded by a lieutenant that in some cases, possessed only an Associate's degree.

After a few years in theatre, the enlisted man brought experience from the battlefield, whereas a new officer rotating in brought experience from the classroom and studying war. An argument could be made for either methodology of learning to be a soldier.

Self education carries the same controversial stigma. Those that bravely attempt to better themselves without the "approval" of formal education risk ridicule, scorn, and contempt. The list of successful people that have self educated is impressive indeed. According to selfmadescholar.com, here are a few alumni from the school of self education:

*leading author of science fiction, Ray Bradbury
*computer mogul and CEO, Michael Dell
*co-creator of the Declaration of Independence, Ben Franklin
*movie director James Cameron

Fear not, self educators, you are in good company in your quest for the Next Level. Out of the methods that I later outline in this book for skill building, formal education is but one path. There are many others if this way does not work for you. The fact of the matter remains: Some people cannot benefit from formal education! The reasons range

The Next Level: SUPERCHARGED

from learning disabilities to a mental aversion to research. Regardless of one's attitudes, it is more important to focus on the method that *does* appeal to the alternative learner. At 19, I could not focus on electronic studies. I went to two schools and just couldn't concentrate on what I needed to learn.

At 26, one of my first jobs upon leaving the Air Force was as an Electronics instructor! What changed? While I was in the military, I spent a lot of time using several of the Next Level principles to compensate for my previous failures. By showing you a variety of learning methods, you may find success where previously you may have only known failure. This is my goal for this book.

At 37, I started reading voraciously. I lucked out and found an amazing book called The Millionaire Mind. As a guy that had read 3 grades above his level throughout elementary school, yet failed out of high school and two colleges, I have always wondered why my mind functions differently than most. I have been called stupid by a LOT of people. Trust me, after awhile, you start to believe it. And you become mediocre.

This book turned out to be a godsend. The author profiled hundreds of people that were millionaires and compiled stats on their education, habits, investments, early academic performance, and degrees earned. The real value of the book was when I got to a chapter discussing a psychologist named Sternberg who had speculated that the human brain is usually divided into one of three types as far as problem solving.

*Analytical- these are your logical test takers that are effective at solving problems that have only one answer. These are your pre-med students and future lawyers that crave structure and very little autonomous control over their careers

The Next Level: SUPERCHARGED

*Practical- these learners are good at thinking on their feet. They can be placed in a completely foreign environment and not just survive, but thrive, i.e. "street smarts"

*Creative- these learners are the ones that can come up with multiple solutions to a problem and are most likely to create things like songs, books, products, websites, and pretty much anything that can be sold. They are typically not good at tests, and struggle at formal, structured education.

They also tend to not do well in high school. They are most likely, however, to become entrepreneurs and CEOs. Why? They have no fear of rejection and will take much larger risks. These were also matching the descriptions of a very high degree of the millionaires profiled in the book.

This last group hit me like a punch in the face. I never took my SATs, yet despite failing out of three different schools, managed to start my own company, write two books, create a clothing line, a skateboard line, and upon being left alone to manage my education, got a PhD. So wait, now it seems that not only am I NOT stupid, but I might be gifted, and have a higher propensity for economic freedom?

> **Dr. Rob's notes:**
> Remember that aptitude is NOT measured with any standardized test! Its perfectly ok to not be a "good" test taker! I am living proof.

I'll buy that for a dollar.

How many other gifted students are out there, shunned by the formal education system that tells them, "If you don't finish college, you are worthless!" How many future Bill Gates or Steve Jobs-level CEOs might never be discovered if they aren't allowed to self educate and learn?

The Next Level: SUPERCHARGED

THAT is why I wrote this book. Self education is valuable. The last year of my life has been my most exciting. I'm still working my goofy day job but I read every day, I am learning about new concepts in exercise, and wealth building. I highly encourage my readers to build themselves mentally and physically, every day if possible.

The Next Level: SUPERCHARGED

The Next Level: SUPERCHARGED

Chapter 4:

The GMOSC (Garcia Model of Skills Comprehension)

The Next Level: SUPERCHARGED

Now that we have discussed the key concepts of this book and seen firsthand how self education takes place, it is time to unveil the central tool that will be pivotal to taking you to the Next Level. The GMOSC Model is a diagram that is used to place a person within a certain level within their desired skill or career. I wanted to create something that was easy to use and visually appealing to the reader.

The GMOSC has five levels from Awareness to Expert. Each of them has certain characteristics that the reader can use to compare their own experiences to self assess. I have also included educational equivalents to give the reader a comparison. I have also included a checklist of questions so that if the reader is stuck between two levels, they can narrow their scope.

For a person to begin, they must first be aware of the existence of the skill or career they are trying to place themselves into. Seems fairly obvious, doesn't it? Well, if you had asked me what a technical writer was when I was 18, I wouldn't have had any idea. The position was undiscovered in my mind at the time. Once I began entering the field at 30, I entered the first skill level: **Awareness**.

Awareness means quite literally, that I was aware of the existence of this job. I was very new to it, had very little experience at what it entailed, and if asked, could only provide a vague explanation of what it meant to be a technical writer.

After I had been at the job a few months, I transferred to a different company. Now, I had the experience of two technical writing positions and I had reached the Next Level: **Familiarity**. Familiarity entailed that I could understand the expectations of the job and with supervision, get significantly harder jobs done. I wasn't qualified to train new employees or create content on my own, but I had a decent grasp of the position.

After a few years, I got hired at a third company as a technical writer and learned far more quickly than I had at

The Next Level: SUPERCHARGED

the previous jobs. I attribute this to the Next Level concepts that I adopted. These concepts will be addressed later in the book. Despite the fact that this third job was far more technically complex,
my learning curve was reduced quite a bit due to the help of Next Level concepts. I can safely say that I met my Next Level yet again and consider myself at the third level: **Proficiency**.

I can make this self assessment because I train new employees, can create content that is used at my job, and if I needed to, could supervise a shift.

This example I have provided is how the GMOSC is to be used. There are two steps for using this book properly: self assess using the GMOSC, and choose 1-10 learning methods provided to improve your skills/career. There is no confusing verbiage, no excessively difficult steps.

So how would I know when I have reached my Next Level? I would read the description of what is expected at the **Mastery** level and work towards being the person described. In my specific case, I would be able to work on any chapter in the manuals we create, would have a far more complex understanding of our work databases, and could intelligently discuss multiple projects with clarity and a high degree of technical comprehension.

The final level, **Expert**, would require roughly 15 years in my career field, hundreds of procedures written, and contributions to trade journals in the field. I don't expect to hit this level, but I do know what it would take. That's the theory behind the GMOSC model. Creating awareness for self assessment. Take a look at the GMOSC and see where you fall in your skill/job:

The Next Level: SUPERCHARGED

Awareness
*Recognition of subject
*Vague knowledge of subject at most basic level
*Knows of existence

Familiarity
*Can describe basic concepts of subject
*Understands subject with some level of certainty
*Understands lowest levels of subject structure
*Able to perform simple tasks related to subject with assistance
*Workplace equivalent of "trainee" or "intern"
*Formal education equivalent of Associate's degree

Proficiency
*Can accomplish tasks related to subject unsupervised
*Able to draw and describe key points of subject with a high degree of comprehension
*Has knowledge of subject from a few years of immersion in topic
*Workplace equivalent of "Journeyman" or "Supervisor"
*Can instruct others in topic
*Formal educational equivalent of Bachelor's degree

Mastery
*Skilled at comprehensive breakdown at every level of topic
*Can perform task at level superior to majority of peers
*Can recite, draw complex diagrams, or perform task at advanced level
*Formal educational equivalent of Master's degree

Expert
*Seen as the highest level of subject matter knowledge
*Can create innovations in the field of specified topic
*Able to produce and implement policy related to topic that is embraced in field
*Formal educational equivalent of Doctoral degree

***Formal educational equivalents are of the author's opinion alone, and are not to be taken as a definitive measure of skill, but rather to create a rough equivalent for clarity of concept.**

The Next Level: SUPERCHARGED

Now that you understand how to use the GMOSC and to take a self assessment, you are ready to learn the 10 learning methods that I have outlined to take you to your Next Level. Feel free to use one, a few, or all of them. As you read through them, think about which ones appeal to your particular learning style and habits.

As a former teacher with many students of various levels of abilities, I learned that the "one size fits all" approach is not only ineffective, it's archaic. Some people learn better from listening, some can only understand something by using their hands, and others will benefit from reading.

How to Use This Book:

1. Identify what you want to learn: (Mandarin/Algebra/Piano/Python Code/Electronics/Long Distance Running/SEO etc......)

2. Rate yourself using the GMOSC on the next page and the descriptions in this chapter

3. Read the 16 methods and choose 2-4 that most match what you are trying to learn

4. Use the worksheets at the end of the book and map out your learning plan using the methods you created

The Next Level: SUPERCHARGED

GMOSC

EXPERT
*Highest Level of Subject Matter Knowledge
*Able to Produce Policy In Field

MASTER
*Skilled at Breakdown of Every Level of Topic
*Performs Tasks FAR Above Peers

PROFICIENT
*Can Instruct Others in Topic
*Can Accomplish Unsupervised Tasks Related to Subject

FAMILIAR
*Can Describe Basic Concepts
*Understands Lowest Level of Subject Structure

AWARENESS
*Recognition of Subject
*Vague Knowledge at Basic Level

The Next Level: SUPERCHARGED

Chapter 5: Learning Method 1 (Research)

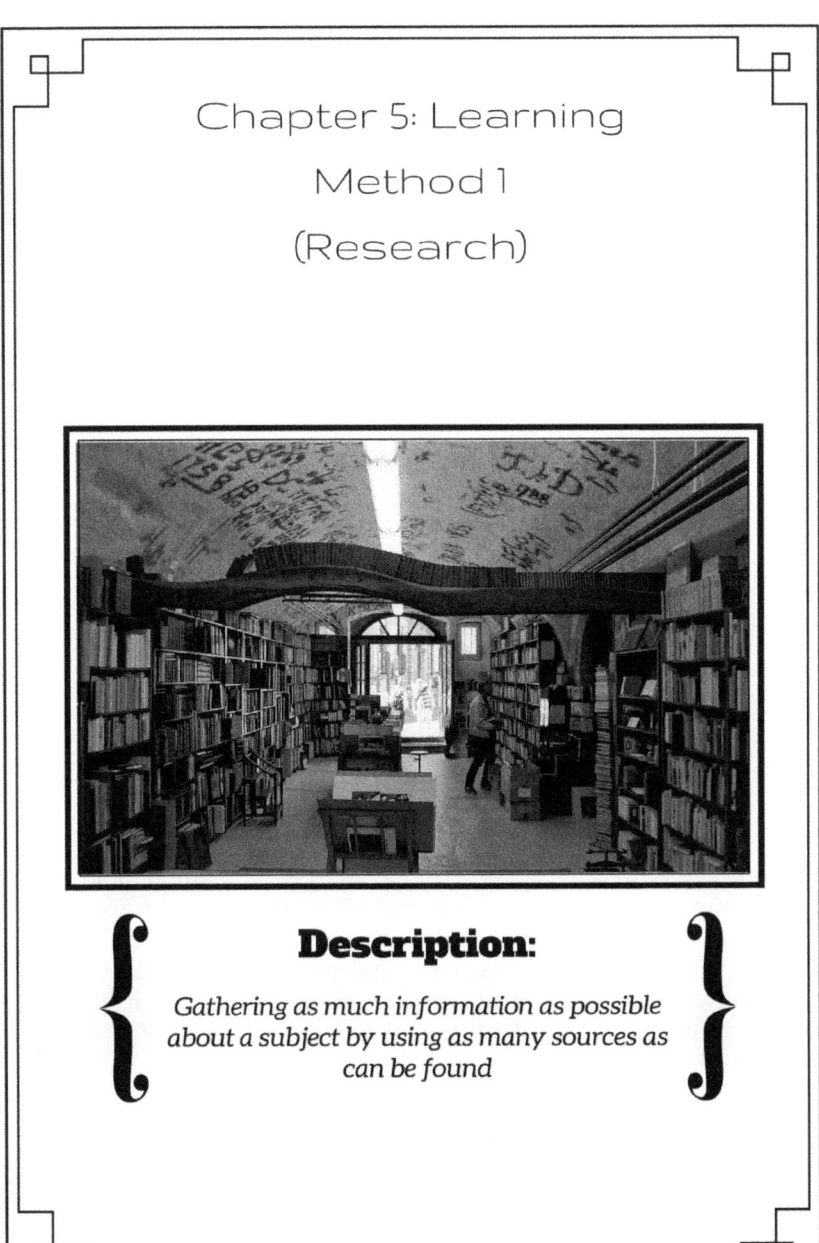

Description:

Gathering as much information as possible about a subject by using as many sources as can be found

The Next Level: SUPERCHARGED

Advantages:

Gives the learner a far more wide reaching spectrum of knowledge than contemporaries. Learner will delve into several categories of subject such as history, experts in field, modern advances and applications, learner will see how topic is viewed from many perspectives

Disadvantages:

High amounts of time required, learners with aversions to reading/scholarly research and analysis will be apprehensive, learner needs to have a strong desire of knowledge for this method

Most Likely Practitioners:

Visual learners
Analytical/logical personalities
Social introverts due to prevalence of independent actions

Overview:

Research involves heavy reading, analysis of material, and a desire to gather from many sources on the desired topic. A learner that uses research as a learning method will embark on a journey of self discovery and resource gathering. The crafty researcher will realize that research can also involve live subjects or observation, not just doing Google searches and going to the library.

Many career fields have embraced research as a way to advance their comprehensive knowledge at their particular specialty. In some cases, research is essential to growth and advancement. Without embracing the current body of knowledge, any type of career or skill improvement is nearly impossible.

The Next Level: SUPERCHARGED

The first example I will use is the archeologist. Their careers are based upon studying ancient civilizations and cultures. A successful archeologist must be an effective researcher in order to seek out relevant information for the culture they are studying. Can you imagine an archaeological dig overseas that was not researched, planned, or organized? It would be a stunning failure.

Archeology is a very important career field because many uncovered sites can become tourist attractions that can generate revenue for decades. Besides the potential for income, the practices of ancient civilizations can teach us about their technology, irrigation methods, religions of the day, and even day to day life.

An archeologist's job begins in the library. Before field work can be planned out, an archeologist must use research to learn everything they can about the desired culture to be examined. Geography, history, even seasonal migration must be studied in order to properly design an archeological dig. Research plays a crucial role in this field and by the time research is finished, the archeologist has gained a "day in the life" perspective of their subject of study.

The next field that uses research extensively is law enforcement, particularly detectives. When a detective is assigned a particularly difficult case, they must "reconstruct the crime", they examine every variable they can, interview as many people as possible, and must be meticulous in evidence collection. They must also have a working knowledge of the parameters of the law within their city and state.

I was particularly moved by one particular case that was researched for this book. Larry Kot and Brion Hanley were given a case that involved a missing girl whose body was later found. The killer was never brought to justice. The case, while having some promising

The Next Level: SUPERCHARGED

leads had reached a standstill and remained open. What made it even more challenging................was that the abduction had occurred in 1957.

The pair immediately started to recreate the timeline of events, set up a suspect list of immediate friends and family, and set out to interview the surviving witnesses. What impressed me most was the level of dedicated data collection that the detectives used to narrow down the possible suspects.

The detectives literally had to recreate the entire event, research every pertinent variable, such as timelines for alibis, to travel times of suspects to weather patterns for the evening. After months of meticulous research and footwork, they presented enough evidence, physical and circumstantial, to enable prosecutors to arrest a neighbor that had a long history of criminal offenses against women. Their hard work solved a 55 year mystery and gave closure to the abducted girl's family.

Think about how much this helped advance their careers. These detectives can take the framework, practices, and experience of solving this case and apply it to future work. They can write books about it, advance their professional knowledge, and will be viewed as experts in their field for solving such a daunting case. In this particular example, the results of their research had the potential to raise them to their Next Level.

Whereas detectives use research to recreate the events of the past, what about using research to create the events of the future? Military strategists employ research techniques to plan military operations, wars, rescue missions, and more. A military strategist must examine every possible variable, potential outcome, current intelligence estimates of opposing forces, if applicable, and more.

For a major operation such as Enduring Freedom or Operation Iraqi Freedom, strategists work for months, if not years, to create a sequence of events that involve the

The Next Level: SUPERCHARGED

symbiosis of logistics, force shaping, possible scenarios, casualty estimates, and eventually, an exit strategy. Strategists must go further than troop lists and equipment tables. They must study cultural norms for the host country, weather patterns, and even the time of year for an optimal mission. All of this must be researched and carefully annotated.

According to the UK National Archives, D-Day, the Allied invasion, took nearly a year to plan. Strategists had to find an area that was lightly defended, allocate resources to produce boats for transportation, interact with friendly countries to align forces, and keep the whole operation a secret so that Germany would not learn the invasion details and reinforce the area. The overwhelming success of the Normandy invasion is a testament to the importance of accurate and long term research.

> Dr. Rob's notes:
> One of the reasons napoleon had so many victories was that he was a meticulous researcher. before a battle he knew weather and tide conditions, the opposing army's weapons and the habits of the opposing commanders.

Best Practices:

You have now seen the power of research in action. This important learning method can quickly ascend you to your Next Level, if you have the time to properly use it. You'll need time, attention to detail, and a willingness to go the extra mile to gather data.

The Next Level: SUPERCHARGED

The University of Chicago Library website offers the following tips for using research effectively:

*Identify and document your topic

*Conduct background research/analysis

*Determine the type of info you need

*Plan your search strategy

*Evaluate results

The Next Level: SUPERCHARGED

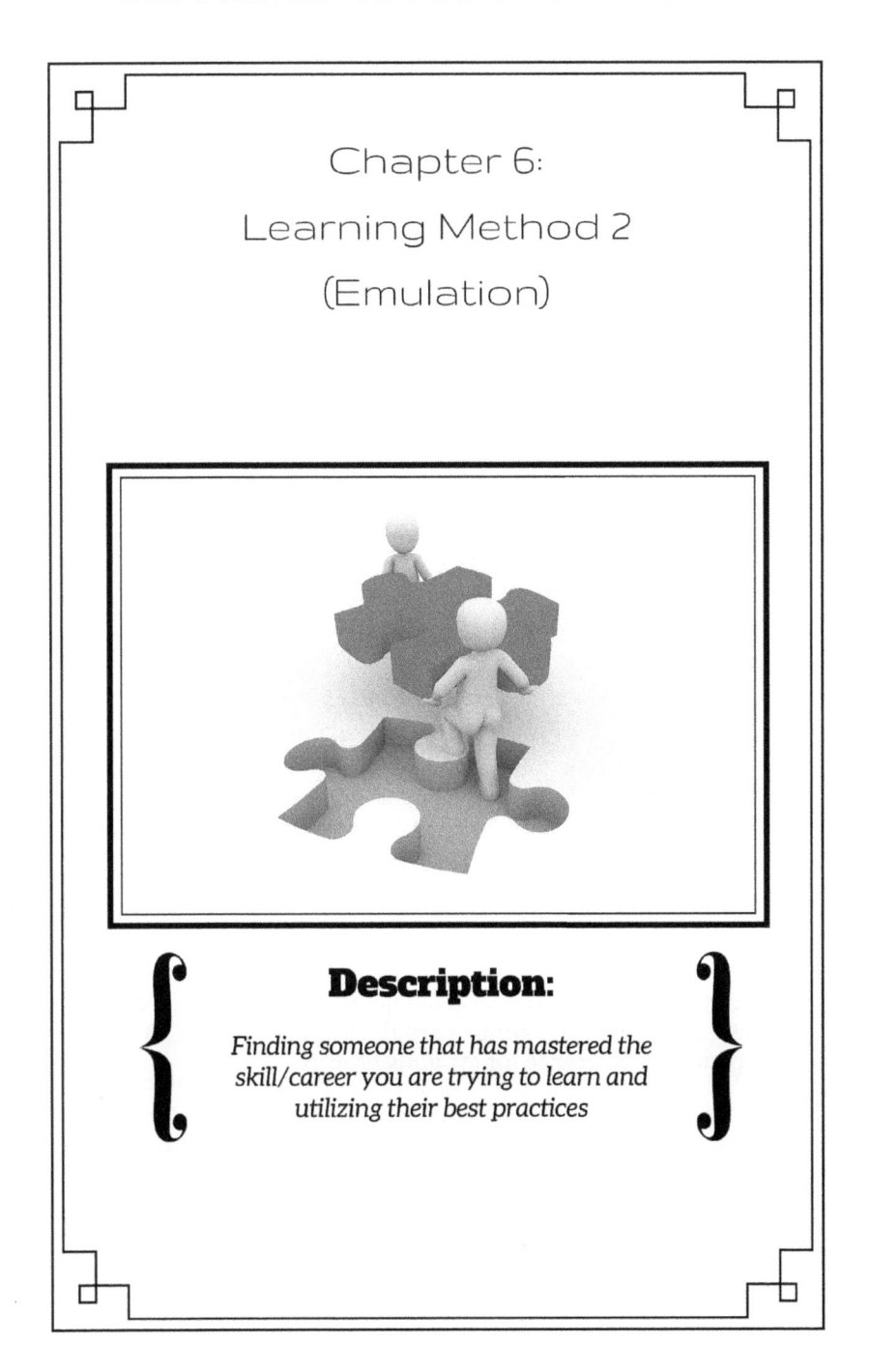

Chapter 6:
Learning Method 2
(Emulation)

Description:

Finding someone that has mastered the skill/career you are trying to learn and utilizing their best practices

The Next Level: SUPERCHARGED

Advantages:

Provides path for success that has been proven to work at least once, gives specific steps to guide the learner, seeing someone successful at your desired skill/career can provide motivation

Disadvantages:

Risk of being seen as a plagiarist/copycat, possible alienation/hostility towards "imitators"

Most Likely Practitioners:

All learners

Overvew:

Emulation follows the old adage of, "what one can do, another can do better." The learner finds someone, alive or dead, that is considered an expert in their skill/career and starts to compile the practices, habits, and ideas of that person in order to achieve their own style of actions.

One of the most famous examples of emulation is Thomas Edison. As a young child growing up in a low income family, Edison had many academic difficulties in school. He was also suffering from partial deafness, which would explain his preference for avoiding crowds.

Edison was a very inquisitive child and would often annoy his teachers by asking so many questions. His mother encouraged his thirst for knowledge and supported his attempts at self learning. At this point, he had acquired an interest in chemistry and physics. He obtained a copy of Newton's Principia, which only emboldened him further. After reading the Principia, he understood the physics

The Next Level: SUPERCHARGED

concepts within it, but despised the formal and dry delivery of the material. Edison believed in simplicity of learning.

Edison would take Newton's findings and observations and apply them to his own experiments in his lab. By emulating the discoveries that Newton had made decades earlier, Edison went on to create hundreds of invention related to sound recording, and light and electricity generation.

Emulation sounds like a form of copying, and if done incorrectly, it is. Emulation should be *your own actions and results based on using previously discovered knowledge, skills, and findings*. It is very important to give credit if you are emulating someone or using a previous discovery for your own gain.

Many times in academia, a student or professor has gotten in hot water for "borrowing" a passage or work from someone and not citing the source properly. This is called *plagiarism* and can lead to expulsion, loss of reputation, or in some cases, termination of employment. Always make sure to make it known when you are crossing into someone's intellectual territory.

In the workplace, the person to emulate is not necessarily the highest ranking person or the boss, but the person *whose career path you most want to follow*. If someone has been at the job for a long time, the advice I always received was to take them to lunch, and pick their brain. Ask questions about how to better your performance, work habits that are helpful, mistakes they have made, and resources they use.

The main reasons that we wish to emulate others?

1. They have a life you perceive as better than yours
2. To attain their degree of success
3. To use them as a platform for *your* degree of success
4. To achieve and *surpass* their achievements

The Next Level: SUPERCHARGED

When we emulate someone we are trying to gather some or all of the following:

- **Their level of comprehension** (When presented with a dilemma, how do they solve it? Do they understand new concepts right away?)

- **Their habits** (What do they do as soon as they get to work? Are they punctual? Do they arrive before anyone else?)

- **Their level of performance** (Are they constantly outperforming their peers? Do they consistently beat records and achievements of others?)

- **Their resources** (What software are they using? What do they have in their office to help them do their job? If they have a talent, what resources are they often using?)

- **Their results** (How can you be competitive/equal/superior to them?)

- **How they achieve their successes while mitigating failures** (Do they "bounce back" quickly when faced with a setback? How do they cope with rejection/failure/catastrophic loss?)

- **Their professional practices** (Are they involved in networking? Publishing in their field? Advancing their chosen field of study?)

- **Their routine** (What is their day like? What are they consistently doing to achieve success? What are the most expected actions for them to do?)

- **Their analytical/decision making process** (How do they disseminate and categorize large pieces of information? How do they use logic to decide their next course of action? What process do

The Next Level: SUPERCHARGED

they use to weigh various business decisions against each other?)

- **Their status/stature in life** (Where are they in relation to you in income/living situation/personal success/relationships?)

Best Practices:

In order to emulate someone effectively, the following steps should be taken:

- Observation (Watch them carefully and observe body language or practices while they are working/using skill to be emulated. What patterns emerge?)

- Inquiry (Ask them directly. Most people are flattered that someone would want to work/perform/achieve like them.)

- Practice (Once you have isolated certain habits/traits to emulate, try them out for yourself and see if you increase your effectiveness.)

- Accumulation of Resources (Find out what they use to perform/work/achieve the desired results/output to be emulated. Can you acquire these same resources for your own personal growth?)

- Fine Tuning (Once you have tried their practices/habits, which ones showed promise? Which ones weren't successful? Adjust accordingly.)

- Setting a Level of Expectation (Are you attempting to be as effective as this person? Better? Or are you trying to just show improvement at *your* own level of performance? Its always better to have a desired result or outcome in mind beforehand.)

The Next Level: SUPERCHARGED

The Next Level: SUPERCHARGED

Chapter 7: Learning Method 3 (Tutelage)

Description:

To find a mentor or guide to instruct in the desired skill/career

The Next Level: SUPERCHARGED

Advantages:

Learner receives direct instruction from a seasoned professional, gains personalized attention

Disadvantages:

Instruction is limited to mentor's scope of experience and knowledge, difficult to locate experts at some obscure skills

Most Likely Practitioners:

Auditory and Kinesthetic learners

Overvew:

Students throughout history have benefited from the help of a dedicated mentor. The correct guidance can be helpful to a learner because they have a direct source to address inquiries to, a pool of knowledge to draw from, and can solicit immediate feedback or criticism for performance.

One of the earliest mentor/student relationships occurred between Socrates and Plato. Socrates at the time, was one of the most well known philosophers in Athens, Greece. (So well known in fact, that one of the Learning Methods in this book is based off of his famous Socratic Method of questioning.)

During this time, Socrates was 50 years older than Plato, and giving direct instruction to many young people in Athens. Socrates believed strongly in self reflection and growth. He devoted his life to enlightening others. In fact, it was his practice of mentoring that led to his famous trial and untimely death (thank goodness, mentors are better regarded these days).

The Next Level: SUPERCHARGED

Plato eventually took the teachings of Socrates and opened his own lecture hall in which he taught the philosophic principles of his beloved mentor. This is one of the greatest tributes I have ever read about concerning a strong mentor/student relationship. In this way, Socrates' teachings and philosophies lived on through the actions of his favorite student.

On a personal note, when I decided to start hardest thing I have ever done, Doctoral studies at University of Phoenix, they required the use of a mentor and a committee in order to guide me along the path to a PhD in Education. My mentor, Dr. Samuel Hardy, was one of the most patient men I ever met. He was on the East Coast and I was on the West, but he always got my revisions done and back quickly. I lost count of the red pens he must have gone through correcting my paper. My program, which was supposed to be 4 years, stretched to 6.5. Still, Dr. Hardy stuck around and so did my committee members.

The importance of what they did can never be repaid, but I will try. I am currently mentoring 5 people and I never charge. I appreciate that they value my advice. Once you get to Proficient or higher, I HIGHLY recommend becoming a mentor. It's a great feeling, and it increases your own skill. When a protégé asks a question that I don't have an immediate answer for, I look it up and check the answer against 3-5 sources.

Finding a Good Mentor

So now that you understand the advantages of a mentor, your next question is: How the heck do I find one? There are several methods for locating someone that can help you reach your next level. If it a mentor for a career path, I would suggest using the website Linkedin.

You can search out people by their careers and buzzwords in their profile. Send them a message explaining

The Next Level: SUPERCHARGED

that you are trying to better yourself in a career and ask them politely if they would mind mentoring you in that field.

Another way to find a mentor in a career field is to Google the skill and throwing in some key words to narrow the search. If you are looking for a mechanic, for example, try the following:

"skilled mechanic"
"award winning mechanic"
"certified mechanic"

By using buzzwords, you create a search that will separate the average from the noteworthy. Once you get a list going, email them.

If you are trying to improve in a skill, same method applies. Google the skill, throw in buzzwords and see what comes up.

Another mistake that we tend to make is discounting geographic propinquity. Your mentor could be in Europe, China, South America or anywhere in the world. The internet has literally given you access to the majority of people on Earth. Don't be narrow minded in your thinking and don't assume that just because someone is in another country that there will be a language barrier. Many countries require English as well as their home language. Don't fall victim to limited thinking.

Mentor Etiquette

So you landed a mentor and they have agreed to help you in your endeavors. Great job! Here are a few tips to make sure that you both maximize the professional relationship:

*Remember at the beginning to CLEARLY communicate your needs. What are your expectations? Weekly progress

The Next Level: SUPERCHARGED

checks or sessions? Monthly? Do you have a time frame in mind? How long until you reach self sustenance?

*Be sure to respect your mentor's time. Odds are, if they are accomplished in their field, they are pretty busy. Do NOT bother them with multiple calls, emails, or texts. The mentor/protégé relationship is a subservient one. In plain English, *they don't need you, you need them.* Remember that and act accordingly.

*It is highly recommended that you do something nice if someone does volunteer to mentor you. Starbucks card, mow their lawn, Bed, Bath and Beyond gift certificate, whatever.

*Another thing to note. If your mentor gives you direct advice and you don't follow it, you better have a DAMN good reason that you didn't take it. I have a few of my protégés that still insist on doing things "their way" which is fine, but once I see them repeatedly going against my advice and failing, it makes me want to limit my time with them. A mentor isn't always right, but if you aren't willing to follow advice from someone more experienced, why the hell are you using a mentor anyway?

Best Practices:

*Locate your mentor and when they agree to help you, establish a routine and expectations from both of you

*Check in regularly, but not too much. If a few weeks go by, its ok to follow up with a polite email

*Use their experience to ask questions and to find out what to do and NOT to do in your search for the Next Level

The Next Level: SUPERCHARGED

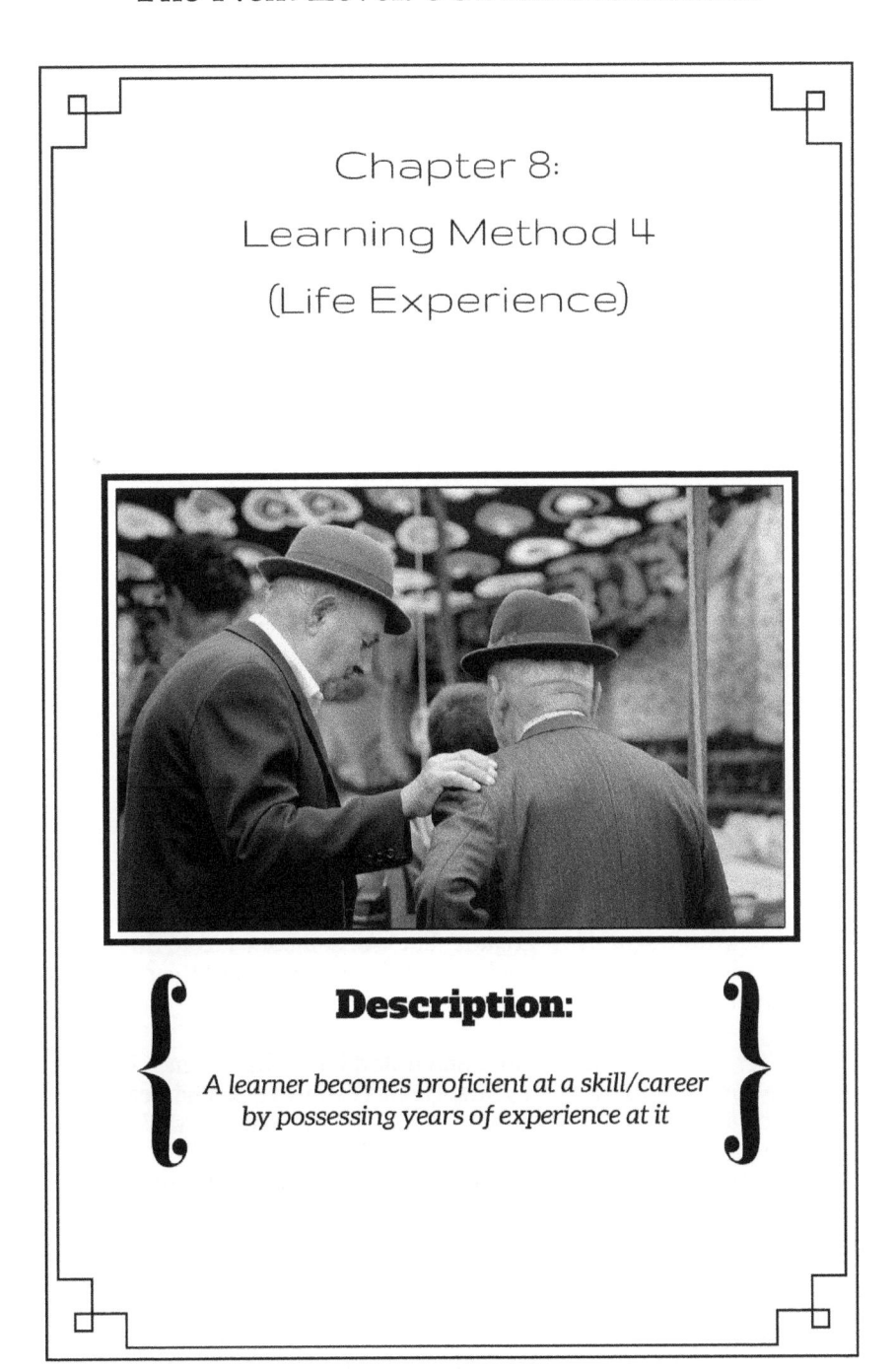

The Next Level: SUPERCHARGED

Chapter 8:
Learning Method 4
(Life Experience)

Description:

A learner becomes proficient at a skill/career by possessing years of experience at it

The Next Level: SUPERCHARGED

Advantages:

Learner will be prepared for obstacles and major changes in career/skill due to lived experiences and observed occurrences, does not necessarily require formal education, mostly observation and patience

Disadvantages:

Requires learner to devote time to acquire experience, must weather ups and downs of staying in the same field or practicing skill

Most Likely Practitioners:

Self directed learners

Overvew:

      This is one of the most passive ways of achieving the Next Level several times, but requires years of commitment. A person that has been in a career for 10+ years is regarded as the "go to" person, *usually regardless of actual, measurable skill*. How great is that? All someone has to do is <u>exist</u> in a career or engage in a skill for a decade and they are perceived as competent and experienced.

      I work with a guy named Jerry that has been with the company for over 20 years. He has extensive mechanical knowledge from his time in the Navy and his years of work in the civilian sector. Jerry is easily at the Master level on the GMOSC and I don't even know if he finished college! He walks around with an air of authority and everyone respects him immediately.

      His commitment to staying in one field and learning as much as he can, easily places him above Proficient in the GMOSC. Listening to him, you realize that he has seen a

The Next Level: SUPERCHARGED

multitude of changes in the company, from the designs of the turbines we use, to the advent of the Internet, to the diagnostic tools we run.

Jerry has literally decades of firsthand experience in hydro mechanical technology and is highly valuable to the company because of it.

So now that you are committed to this career, what are a few ways to maximize your habits? Using your resources of course.

Quick question, what's the most valuable resource at your work?

People.

Too many people lose track of this asset and just think of resources as tangible items related to office supplies and computers. At my work, our building is nothing but tech writers in one small corner and engineers. Lots of engineers. You'd think that they would interact a lot, go out socially, and maximize each other for success.

This isn't the case. It's almost like being in high school again. Both groups only use each other when it's necessary to get a job done. I saw this in my first few weeks and decided to take a stand in order to improve my work environment. Every morning, when I get coffee in the break room and I see someone I don't know, I ask them about their education, their family, and their time with the company.

A funny thing happened. People started waving at me when they walked by my cube. I started getting lunch invites, and making new friends. And guess what? When I am writing a procedure and have a question, I have ten new friends that all have their own engineering specialty and expertise. Think that's valuable in helping me to achieve my own Next Level?

You bet.

The Next Level: SUPERCHARGED

Best Practices:

*Commit to a skill or career and plan for the long haul

*Use your resources wisely and keep up with changes in technology and staffing

*Engage in as much professional development and related training as possible

*Make friends. You aren't in high school. You can be an adult and meet new people that you wouldn't normally talk to.

*Accept the fact that you WILL be the first person that gets asked advice. This is a privilege. Be cool about it.

The Next Level: SUPERCHARGED

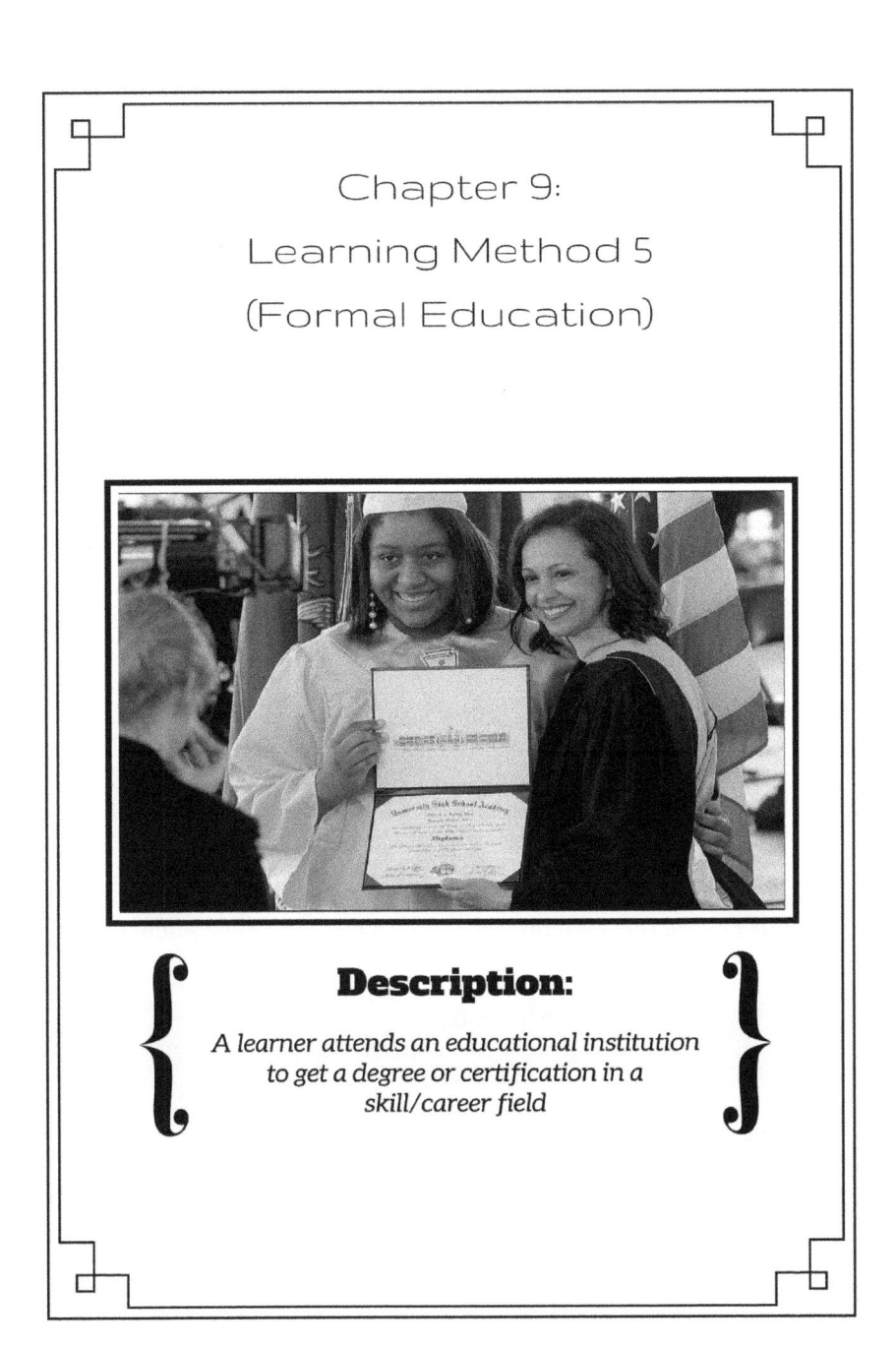

Chapter 9: Learning Method 5 (Formal Education)

Description:

A learner attends an educational institution to get a degree or certification in a skill/career field

The Next Level: SUPERCHARGED

Advantages:

Higher earning potential, viewed as competent in chosen skill/field, academia provides balanced curriculum, opens eligibility for certain technical/specific fields

Disadvantages:

Expensive, requires commitment to educational goals, partial completion doesn't offer many benefits

Most Likely Practitioners:

Analytical thinkers
Confident test takers
Students that aren't afraid of a multi-year commitment

Overvew:

Formal education is a way to achieve your Next Level while reaping several benefits. Before committing to formal education, you must weigh several options. This is one of the most intensive methods described in this book. It can be very expensive, take a long period of time, and is not guaranteed. Why choose this method? Here are some of the most popular reasons:

1. Higher income potential
2. Acknowledgement from family/friends
3. Sense of accomplishment
4. Life goal
5. Elevated status in life
6. Higher self perception
7. Stand out in a crowd of applicants

Keep in mind that formal education is very controversial. Some people will tell you it is a complete waste of time, others will tell you that getting a degree is essential.

The Next Level: SUPERCHARGED

I currently have six degrees. Two Air Force AAs, an AA and BS in Pro Aero, an MBA and an Ed.D from University of Phoenix (PhD for Education). Here are some gathered observations:

1. The majority of people that talk down about formal education are those without degrees.
2. Having a degree is an earned privilege. It is NOT an excuse to talk down to people.
3. I have interviewed with 2 Fortune 500 companies and my education not only made me competitive, it got me hired at both!
4. My boss doesn't even look at resumes that do not contain completion of a Bachelor's degree.
5. The majority of people do NOT work in the field that they obtained a degree in.

Here is an interesting fact about getting a Bachelor's degree. In many formal organizations, a Bachelor's makes you eligible for hire, *no matter what subject it is in*. In a nutshell, that degree in Philosophy or History can get your foot into any of the following:

1. CIA agent
2. FBI agent
3. Military Officer
4. Dept of Homeland Security
5. State Dept
6. Eligibility to apply to Law School

Rating a School's Value

For this section, I will be honest. I'm going to give my opinion, not justifiable fact. Take it with a grain of salt and feel free to cross reference with other sources. The value of a degree falls upon the following:

1. School's reputation
2. Level of integration in desired career field

The Next Level: SUPERCHARGED

3. Perception of degree to job recruiter
4. Rigor of schoolwork and projects

Education is expensive. When you are choosing a program and school, keep in mind that when you go for that job interview, what are you going to have? It's very important to find out about the school's accreditation, professional reputation, and how often graduates get matched with employers.

It isn't smart to get a degree in something like journalism at a top name school if you are going to expect a starting salary of $32,000 a year and you will owe $1000 a month in student loans.

If you have questions about a school, or want to know about a certain career field, email me. Ill be happy to give free advice. (Dr. Rob's email: dragonsgold76@gmail.com).

> Dr. Rob's notes:
> Keep in mind that education, intelligence, aptitude, and genius are completely different subjects. I know plenty of people that are educated that cannot figure out simple tasks in real life.

The Next Level: SUPERCHARGED

Types of Degree Groupings

This is a loose interpretation of several popular degree groupings. There are plenty more out there.

Professional:

Education
Architecture
Engineering
Medical
Accounting
Law
Engineering
Business

Technical:

Engineering (fits the description of both technical and professional)
Computer Software

Liberal Arts:

English
Art
Journalism
History
Philosophy
Music

Sciences:

Biology
Geology
Chemistry

The Next Level: SUPERCHARGED

Keep in mind that there are many schools that should be avoided, particularly ones that have issues with their accreditation. For the amount of work that you are investing, your school should meet all your personal criteria. I would always tell you to do something you love, not something to make money. The money and success will follow you if you are passionate, work hard, and become an expert in your field.

Best Practices:

I would honestly use Socratic Method with a friend to isolate why you are going to school and what you expect from it. Some people go for more income, some to make a difference socially, and others just want to be the first in their family to get a degree.

Once you know why you are going, make a list of schools offering the educational program you are seeking. Google the school and find out their accreditation standing and see what people are saying about it. Find out their graduation and placement rate.

The Next Level: SUPERCHARGED

Chapter 10: Learning Method 6 (Repetitive Practice)

Description:

Learner repetitively engages in skill/career until comprehension and sense of ownership occurs

The Next Level: SUPERCHARGED

Advantages:

Learner gathers increased talent from repetition and habit forming, learning curve gets smaller, technique stimulates muscle memory

Disadvantages:

Requires major allocations of learner's time, learners with short attention spans will have trouble with amount of dedication required, ineffective for cross sectional (multi-task) learning

Most Likely Practitioners:

Self directed learners, introverts, actors, musicians, martial artists

Overview:

Repetitive practice is a technique that is applicable to select fields. It requires months, sometimes years, of consistent practice at the desired skill and some careers to master. It is mostly effective with performing arts and theatre work.

This technique is successful because it causes the brain to create new patterns of "muscle memory" from the similarity in movements. The brain learns to perform the task on "autopilot" because of accomplishing it so many times.

This is a great method for actors to memorize lines, for musicians to learn detailed musical pieces, and for martial artists to learn long, difficult forms.

The Next Level: SUPERCHARGED

Best Practices:

Repetitive practice can lead to boredom, especially after hours of the same action. Try to allocate break times to walk around and to not let monotony fester. Remember that you are performing this technique in order to become skilled and to eventually let your brain create patterns so that it becomes easier.

The Next Level: SUPERCHARGED

The Next Level: SUPERCHARGED

Chapter 11: Learning Method 7 (Creation)

Description:

Learner creates item/product/device directly related to skill/career

The Next Level: SUPERCHARGED

Advantages:

Learner has opportunity for name recognition, possible profitability, learner will have "ground up" experience

Disadvantages:

Prototypes are costly, skepticism from existing practitioners in field

Most Likely Practitioners:

Prodigies, high IQ inventors/entrepreneurs

Overview:

Creation is an interesting methodology because it causes the practitioner to actually make a tangible item in their skill/career. The range of items is nearly limitless. I personally have created clothing, branded skateboards, books, and hats. It's a great feeling to have a product line that you personally designed.

Creation can be something simple (I made an Excel program that reminded us when a project was nearing deadline) to complicated (new computer model or engine). You are only limited to cost of materials and imagination. Creation can be a great way to show others your skills and talents. If your item gets popular, you can brand it, and mass produce for
profit. Keep in mind that creation can be a tangible, physical item, or something that is intellectual property such as a website, a song, or software.

One person that used Creation to break into her field successfully was Katrina Lucero. Katrina had always been looking to find her niche in life. She was highly intelligent and could speak Mandarin Chinese, yet wasn't happy in the

The Next Level: SUPERCHARGED

corporate world. She had gained weight and was ready for a new chapter in life. She took a drastic step and got gastric bypass surgery. Within a few months, she had lost a great deal of weight, and had adopted a new gym regiment that contributed to her fitness.

She dreamed of doing fitness competitions but noticed that tattoos weren't allowed on competitors. She had a moment of inspiration and decided that she would start her own fitness magazine. One that exclusively focused on tattooed and body modified competitors. With that, Fitness Inked was born.

She immediately set up photo shoots, looked for outside funding, and recruited staff. Slowly it came together. In three months after its debut, Fitness Inked had nearly 50,000 hits. Katrina received a lot of skepticism and critical comments from people, but didn't let it deter her. Future plans include a print copy launch in 2014, and more modeling shoots.

Other notable folks that used Creation were Bill Gates, Michael Dell, Henry Ford, and Edison.

Dr. Rob's notes:
Creation is one of my personal favorite next level techniques because it brings a learner's aptitude out in the open. make something amazing and the world will marvel at your talents!!

Best Practices:

Creation requires imagination, accumulation of resources, and a plan. Find others that follow your passion and goals, and create the best possible product you can. Look online for similar products, acquire free resources when you are able, and don't let skeptics deter you from your dreams.

The Next Level: SUPERCHARGED

The Next Level: SUPERCHARGED

Chapter 12: Learning Method 8 (Socratic Method)

Description:

Using the art of asking informative questions to solve problems and gather information

The Next Level: SUPERCHARGED

Advantages:

Creates a wide body of knowledge, learner gathers information about skill/career that is far reaching

Disadvantages:

Sources answering questions must be knowledgeable, requires learner to locate sources

Most Likely Practitioners:

    Auditory learners
    Diagnosticians
    Systems Analysts
    Surgeons
    Systems Engineers
    Designers (ergonomic)
    Religious Scholars
    Small Business Owners

Overview:

When in doubt, how about turning to an ancient philosopher? Socratic Method is still practiced in law school today, much to the distaste of many first year students (Google "The Paper Chase Socratic Method Scene" for example). Socratic Method is often misunderstood as a technique of "just asking questions", which is far from the truth.

The Next Level: SUPERCHARGED

Basically, it is a technique of asking sequential questions, receiving a contradictory answer, and then revisiting the question further in order to understand the concept better. The steps go like this:

1. Ask a general question about a topic

2. Receive answer

3. Formulate second question that creates ambiguity or direct contradiction

4. Subject is forced to engage in deeper thought and clarification on subject

5. Higher level of thought and subject understanding is created

Socratic Method was designed to create higher level thought and understanding. It stimulates the user to seek a more developed comprehension of the topic or subject. I have used it as a way to define what my company does, who it serves, and what its goals are. It is a very effective tool. Socratic Method can be applied to either career progression or skill improvement. It's a great way to create the desire for growth, to isolate the motivation behind your desire for improvement, and to genuinely become more of a subject matter expert.

> Dr. Rob's notes:
> A good rule of thumb when using socratic method is to ask how/what/why?

The Next Level: SUPERCHARGED

Here's an example of how I could use it to improve my company, Blue Dragon Enterprises:

Me: How could I make Blue Dragon more successful?

Friend: How do you define success?

Me: Impact on other people's lives, slight profitability, expansion of my services.

Friend: Why do you need a company for that? Couldn't you do it on your own?

Me: A company gets me a wholesale discount, credibility, and a professional image.

Friend: So, since you have those things, how are you matching them to your company's goals and your vision of success?

By doing this repeatedly, I can plot the direction I should take the company, the vision I should have, and revisit the perception I have of it. Socratic Method is really good for helping you with self direction once you have been asked your questions.

Best Practices:

Find a person that understands the concepts of Socratic Method. Explain it if you need to. They don't even have to be an expert in your field, although I recommend someone that is at least knowledgeable. Take notes of what you come up with, once they start a series of questions, you'd be surprised at what your answers will yield.

The Next Level: SUPERCHARGED

Chapter 13: Learning Method 9 (Immersion)

Description:

Learner directly inserts themselves into career/skill, sometimes with zero preparation or training

The Next Level: SUPERCHARGED

Advantages:

Learner directly faces fears and uncertainties related to skills/career, learner begins gathering experience immediately

Disadvantages:

Requires learner to ignore all hesitation, fear, or skepticism, not a good choice for introverts

Most Likely Practitioners:

Aggressive self starters
Sociologists
Anyone that integrates within a foreign culture
Military

Overvew:

    I'll just say it. Immersion is for the brave. It's the fastest way to a make or break moment. It involves direct and immediate action within a new environment. Talk about a potentially unpleasant experience.

    The best real life example I could think of was Jane Goodall, one of the most famous anthropologists of all time. She was fascinated by chimpanzees at a young age and ended up studying them

The Next Level: SUPERCHARGED

at a wildlife facility in Tanzania in 1960. Without a degree, she observed, analyzed, and recorded their behaviors, habits, and patterns.

She was eventually accepted within the chimpanzee community and was an active part of their lives. She made immersion her entire life because it was her passion and the fastest way she could advance in her career. She eventually received her Doctorate and many awards for her groundbreaking work.

Immersion is a very bold and challenging method. One good aspect is that it teaches you immediately whether you can stomach the stress involved with the new skill/career. You will get immediately exposed to the hardships and challenges. For those of you that crave adventure, challenge, and quick thinking, immersion is probably your ticket to your Next Level.

Best Practices:

Find an opportunity to get directly involved in a career that interests you. It may be an internship, and immediate job opening, or a once in a lifetime opportunity. My experience with Immersion went like this. I was looking for a job, and found an opening for a technical writer. I had zero experience at technical writing but had a technical background. I called the company and asked a few questions. I had the interview and the boss told me he needed to consider it.

I rolled the dice and offered to work for free for three days. He hired me on the spot and told me to come in that day. He liked my confidence. I'm not going to lie, I was terrified and the boss was a former Marine. I ended up doing well by listening to his instructions, really figuring out what he wanted, and interacting well with the employees.

It was a small company, and in three months, he offered me a very high ranking position equivalent to vice

The Next Level: SUPERCHARGED

president. I got an offer from a huge company right after so I had to decline. I never forgot how well Immersion worked though, despite my fears. The very fact that I jumped in, worked my butt off, and took the time to learn the cycle of business that we were in, gained me respect and got me close to the boss.

If you can stomach a dynamic new environment and are quick on your feet, Immersion can pay off BIG.

One very interesting person that I know that used Immersion is pro skateboarder Frankie Hill. Frankie was my hero when I started skating in 1990 (yes, I'm old). Frankie grew up in Santa Barbara, and started skateboarding because his home life wasn't fun for him. He practiced every day and completely devoted his life to skating. He started to get skilled at it quickly.

He was picked up by a large company and turned pro. He was in videos, magazines, and was the first skateboarder that did big handrails back in the early days of street skating. Frankie went on to be one of the most recognized and admired street skaters of the early 1990s and is still ripping today. I have some very good news for you. **Frankie Hill provided an interview exclusively for the Next Level!**

I have known Frankie through Facebook, and I ended up designing two shirts featuring him, although we have never met. I was very happy when he agreed to be interviewed for this book and share his thoughts on skill building. Imagine being able to interview your favorite football player or band. It's hard to imagine, but I got lucky and Frank is a cool guy. His interview is featured in a later chapter.

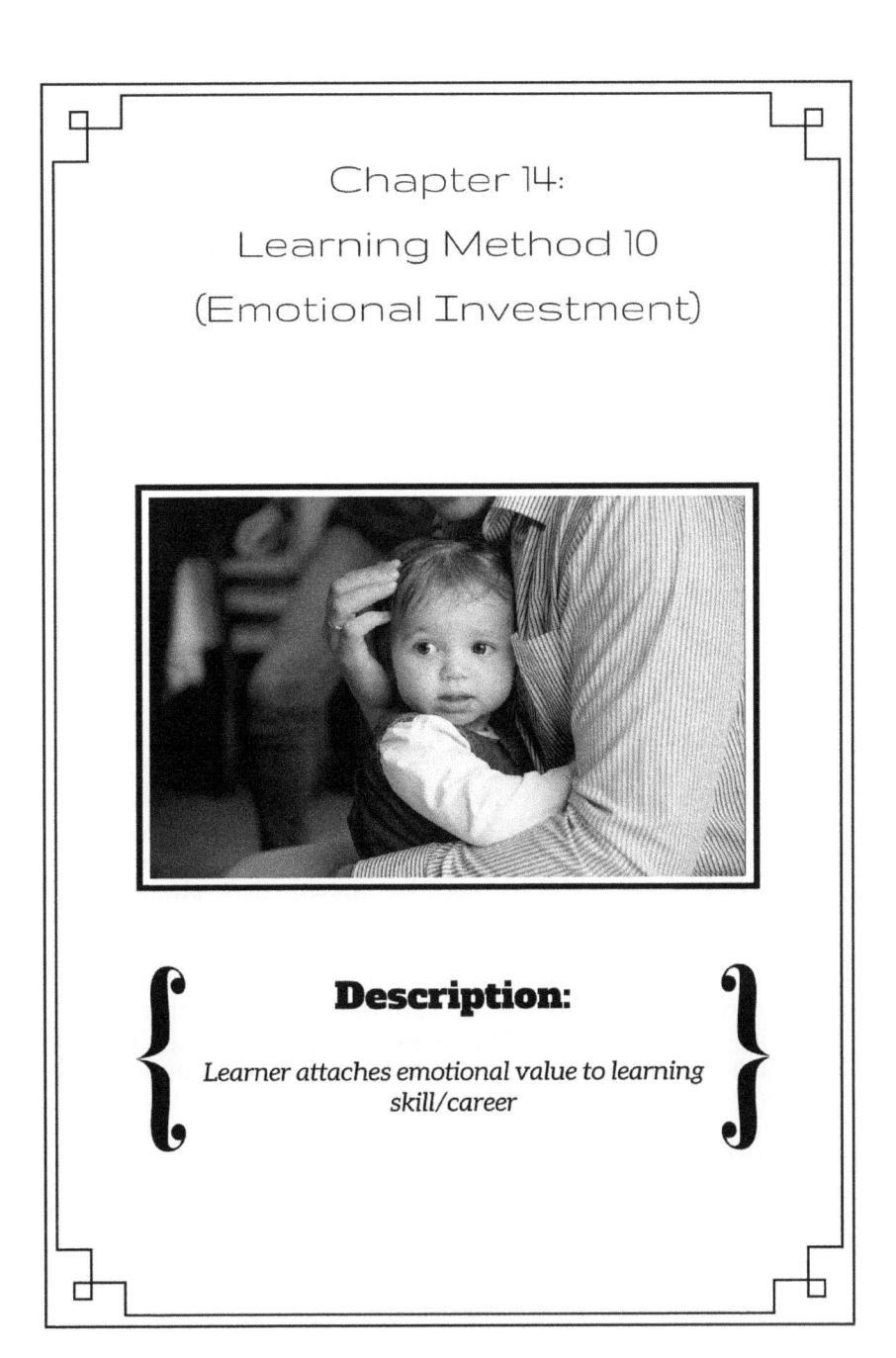

The Next Level: SUPERCHARGED

Chapter 14: Learning Method 10 (Emotional Investment)

Description:

Learner attaches emotional value to learning skill/career

The Next Level: SUPERCHARGED

Advantages:

Much higher level of dedication, learner will stay motivated because of emotional commitment to goals

Disadvantages:

Learner experiences much higher amounts of pressure to perform, failures are viewed as catastrophic

Most Likely Practitioners:

Widows/widowers
Anyone that chose a profession due to loss of relative
Anyone using a tragedy to complete a goal

Overvew:

In life, we endure many trials, some tragic. But can we achieve a Next Level because of it? Emotional Connection is a very powerful methodology for improvement because it causes us to look past ourselves. It makes us achieve because of someone else. We have an investment that is more spiritual, more invested, more committed, than physical. That in itself can be used to produce amazing results.

Some of us have lost a loved one, helped a relative through a grave disease, made a promise to someone special, or just acted on a desire to appease someone close. I got my PhD to prove to myself that despite being brought up in a low income household, moving 14 times before 8th grade, and failing high school once and college twice, that I could do more than I believed.

One of the greatest examples I have ever seen of Emotional Connection being used to achieve amazing things occurred to Dick Hoyt. Dick's son, Richard, was born with cerebral palsy. Doctors and specialists recommended that

The Next Level: SUPERCHARGED

Richard should have been institutionalized, but Dick maintained hope and faith that his son had the potential to be great.

After Dick noticed that Richard's eyes followed him around the room, he realized that Richard had full mental capabilities, despite nearly nonexistent movement. Dick got Richard a computer that was tailored to his condition, and for the first time, they were able to communicate regularly.

After seeing a magazine on racing, Dick and Richard entered a race together, with Richard being pulled. After Richard expressed that it was "like he wasn't handicapped", Dick was a man on a mission. The first few races were rough. Dick was not in shape, and certainly not used to runs involving two people. Yet he persevered. He knew that it created an experience for his son that was unique.

Team Hoyt has now accomplished over a thousand endurance events including six Ironmans. They biked and ran across the US once and completed it in 45 days. Team Hoyt is featured on Youtube and I'm warning you now, you will cry. You will absolutely be overcome with the emotion behind seeing such a display of love and admiration for another person.

I'm very proud to report that Richard completed college at Boston University and set an example for disabled students everywhere. I was even more thrilled when Team Hoyt agreed to be interviewed for the Next Level!! I hope you enjoy reading it as much as I did. Please donate to Team Hoyt. It's a worthy cause.

Another amazing example of using Emotional Connection is Joseph Kapacziewski. I read his book a few months before writing this book and the story is amazing. Joe was a slightly rough around the edges kid growing up on the East Coast in a blue collar family. He didn't feel like he was on the right path, and decided to join the Army.

The Next Level: SUPERCHARGED

While at the recruiter's office, he saw a video that showed the Army Rangers. Joe was hooked immediately. He was a very active, very bold kid and the idea of riding around in helicopters, parachuting, and being the Army's elite caught his attention. He promised to himself that he would not only be a soldier, but a Ranger.

Joe made it through Army Basic Training, Advanced Infantry Training, Airborne School, then Ranger Indoc (now called Ranger Assessment and Selection Period). He was awarded his tan beret and his Ranger scroll. He was in.

As if that wasn't enough, he was approved for Ranger School, which is the hardest light infantry training in the world. Three months of little sleep, minimal food, and high stress situations. To give you an idea of how tough the training is, 27 soldiers have died while attempting to complete it. Joe endured, he kept his sense of humor and graduated. He was now the best of the best. The Rangers are legendary in military circles, and a Ranger Tab means that the wearer has endured some of the hardest land navigation training and combat leadership courses known to man.

Joe was sent on multiple combat tours overseas and on a deployment to Iraq, he was in an armored vehicle when an insurgent grenade flew into an open hatch. Joe was seriously wounded and immediately flown out to receive medical care. He ended up losing his right leg beneath the knee and was fitted with a prosthetic.

Joe endured many painful surgeries and eventually was able to walk again. But the thought of losing his ability to be a Ranger was too much. He had come too far and loved being a Ranger. He craved the excitement, the camaraderie, and the art of soldiering. Joe promised himself that he would not let his injury alter his life. He started a training program that was brutal and challenging.

He petitioned his command and became the first man to be reinstated back to active combat on a prosthetic leg after passing all physical qualifications. Joe's was

The Next Level: SUPERCHARGED

interviewed for the Next Level and he amazed me with his humility despite his amazing achievements. Truly a believer in the power of Emotional Connection. Rangers Lead the Way, indeed.

Best Practices:

If you find yourself setting a goal because of emotional connection, you are taking a huge risk. Make sure that the goal is firmly planted in your mind, your steps are mapped out, and that *you understand when it is complete*.

Try not to set goals out of the desire to prove someone wrong. If you absolutely must do it, be positive about it, and use your goal to help others (I'll just say it: I absolutely am being hypocritical giving this advice. At least I admit it. Most of my goals are the result of proving relatives wrong. I don't advise it and it isn't healthy).

Understand that if you fail to meet your goal, it isn't a total failure. Emotionally connected goals are rough on the body and rougher on the heart. Be ready to mitigate (reduce) the way you view a failure, and reassess if it is worth pursuing again.

I applied to Officer School four times because of the memory of my grandfather. I was denied three of them, and the fourth time I was accepted and a paperwork error that was out of my hands took me out of the running. Think I was disappointed? Oh yeah.

But I'll still apply again soon.

The Next Level: SUPERCHARGED

The Next Level: SUPERCHARGED

Chapter 15:
Learning Method 11
(Masterminds/Groups)

Description:

A group of like minded people that come together to synthesize information and to create new ideas

The Next Level: SUPERCHARGED

Advantages:

Learner receives multiple points of view/synthesis of several high tier thinkers yields much higher results for group. Possible conjuration of "invisible mind."

Disadvantages:

Possible conflicts and potential for disputes. Ego can play a role in disagreements. Finding group members can be time consuming due to need for high performers/results-driven members.

Most Likely Practitioners:

Seekers of knowledge, business owners, entrepreneurs, protégés, mentees, students

Overvew:

The concept of a mastermind group was relatively new to me and I was not aware of its existence until I read The Laws of Success by Napoleon Hill. It has remained a powerful tactic in place for intellectual hyper-growth and the concept of "if one succeeds, we can all succeed."

A mastermind group consists of at least three members and according to The Laws of Success, if done properly, can conjure up an "invisible mind" which sounds like some Harry Potter sorcery, but in reality just means that the participants are elevated to a higher state of thought, as if *another* member of high IQ had joined them.

For a mastermind group to function properly, special care must be taken in selecting the members. This is not an open forum for just any attendee. A mastermind group must be planned and organized like a professional group of experts.

The Next Level: SUPERCHARGED

Best Practices:

The first step should be to make a list of members that would be a good fit for your group. This is where the selection process is key. Members should have one or more of the following traits:

*business owner
*high level of educational accomplishment
*high level of analytical thinking
*well read on current and meaningful topics
*similar life goals and a clear path to achieve them
*optimistic attitude
*supercharged IQ
*has created a "super result" in life
*expert in something
*friendly without arrogance
*creates camaraderie not conflict
*gives more than they ever ask for
*holder of resources
*entrepreneur
*multiple media appearances
*high social value

Once you have created your list of 2-12 other members, plan out the particulars of the meeting. Here are some potential steps:

1. Decide length of meeting and day (2 hours is optimal)
2. Create your itinerary
3. Email members and ask for a firm commitment, if they bust the commitment, they are banned. No exceptions.
4. Decide your venue

Here is a sample itinerary:

2:00pm – 2:15pm Setup and arrangement of laptops/writing devices

The Next Level: SUPERCHARGED

2:15pm - 2:25pm   1 minute introductions (name, occupation, area of specialty)

2:25pm – 2:30pm   Read itinerary of meeting and goals

2:30pm – 3:30pm   Ask the question: "Where are you hitting obstacles in your life goals?" Round Table format. 10 minute limit on discussions and responses

3:30pm – 3:50pm   Ask, "What or who is a great resource for the group?" Round Table

3:50pm – 4pm   Final around the room/closing thoughts

Remember that the goals of a mastermind group are to:

1. Solve Group Issues
2. Create Success For All Members
3. Generate High Tier Thought
4. Network New Members
5. Create Equitable Relationships

The following are **NOT** to be allowed:

1. Gossiping
2. Discussing non agenda items
3. Arguing
4. Denigrating members
5. Flaunting ego
6. Being distracted by side items

It should be noted that for maximum efficiency, you should be a part of THREE categories of groups:

1. In person masterminds with people from meetup.com
2. Online Facebook groups
3. Online Facebook groups that are specific to your goals

The Next Level: SUPERCHARGED

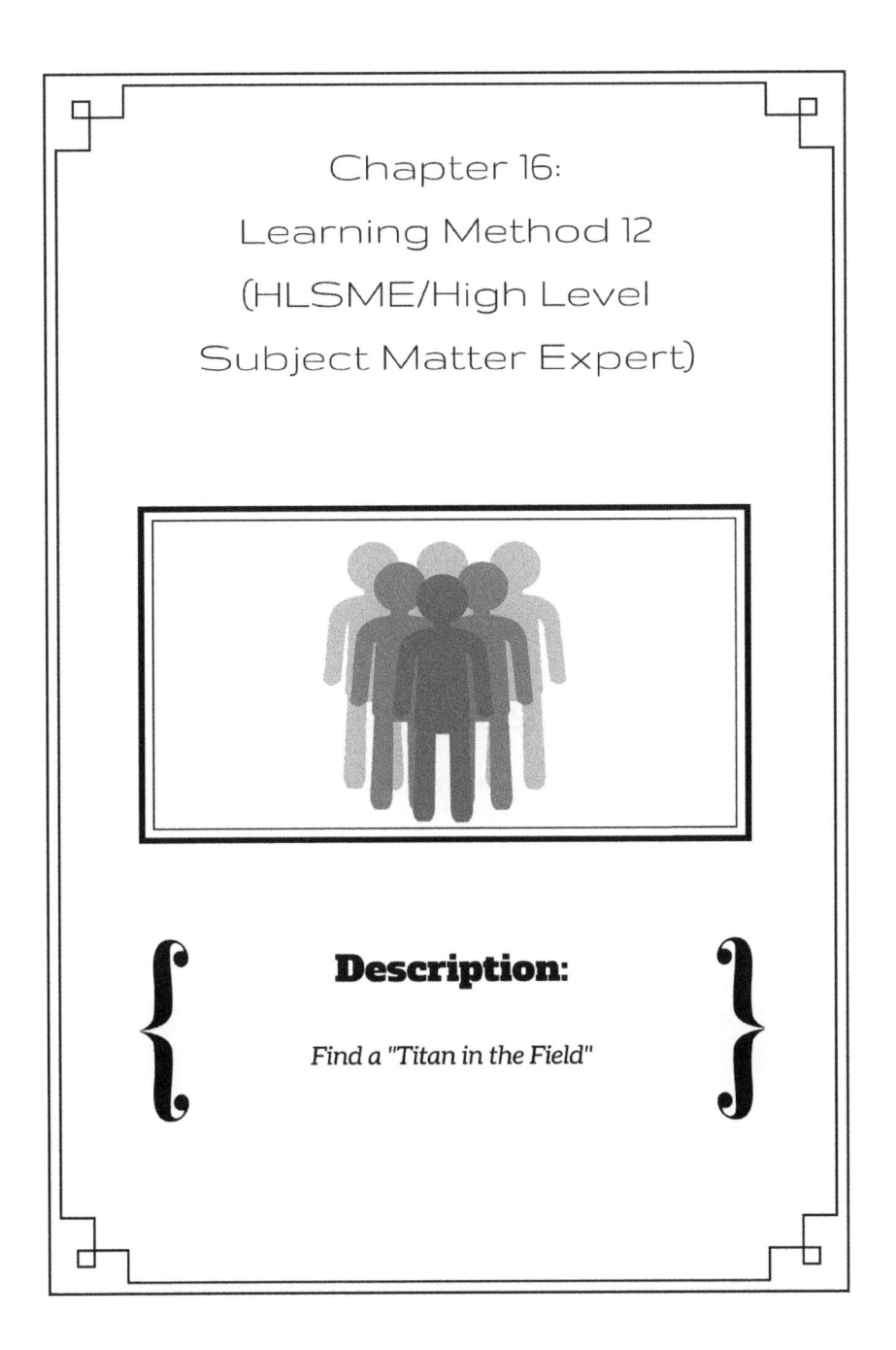

Chapter 16: Learning Method 12 (HLSME/High Level Subject Matter Expert)

Description:

Find a "Titan in the Field"

The Next Level: SUPERCHARGED

Advantages:

HLSME will be able to provide unique and highly valuable advice/lessons on topic

Disadvantages:

Possible difficulty locating them
Some HLSMEs prefer to be left alone
Time constraints can be thin

Most Likely Practitioners:

Students
Young learners
Writers/journalists

Overview:

One of the fastest ways a potential learner can race through the learning process is to locate a HLSME in their desired field of study. Someone that is an expert in the field has many advantages that can be highly beneficial to the learner.

They have mastered the skill or process, they may have authored books or articles on their subject of study, or they may have created something of unbelievable value to their industry.

It is important to know that a HLSME is not the same as a mentor from Chapter 7. A mentor is a far broader category and can include relatives, employers, religious figures, neighbors, pretty much anyone that can guide you.

A HLSME is a SPECIFIC resource in an industry and is well known for their contributions. It is important to realize that contacting one is a tricky and delicate process.

The Next Level: SUPERCHARGED

You will need to be respectful of their time and not be burdensome when asking questions.

What are some criteria for a HLSME?

*Has published articles about their field

*Featured in media/books/podcasts

*Has invented or created ground breaking innovative products

*Teaches in their field

*Has done a TED talk

*Is known in their industry

*Can influence and change policy

So how do we find our expert? There are a few ways, but this process has worked for me:

1. Write down your field and Google it.

2. Take note of articles and websites that pop up. Start taking notes.

3. Next ask a query of Google. Let's say your topic is classic Mustangs. Type in Google, "expert at classic Mustangs" and note the names that appear.

4. Once you have 3-6 names of HLSMEs, it is time to contact them to ask for their assistance. Here are some ways that I have used:

*Facebook

*Linkedin

The Next Level: SUPERCHARGED

*Twitter

*Their business website contact info

*Their management company

*Google their name and "contact info"

Best Practices:

Once you have located contact info, write them a VERY short and to the point inquiry. I'm going to be very specific here.

DO NOT BABBLE

Understand?

They deal with a lot of email traffic every day. They don't need to hear the minute details of your life. All you need to do is explain who you are, what you are working on or trying to do, and how they can best help you.

It will go MUCH better if you drop in a few personal tidbits about their career. This shows that you read about them and actually took the time to find out about them instead of hustling them for free advice. Remember, they DONT need you. You need them. So be respectful and keep the interactions on their terms, not yours.

The Next Level: SUPERCHARGED

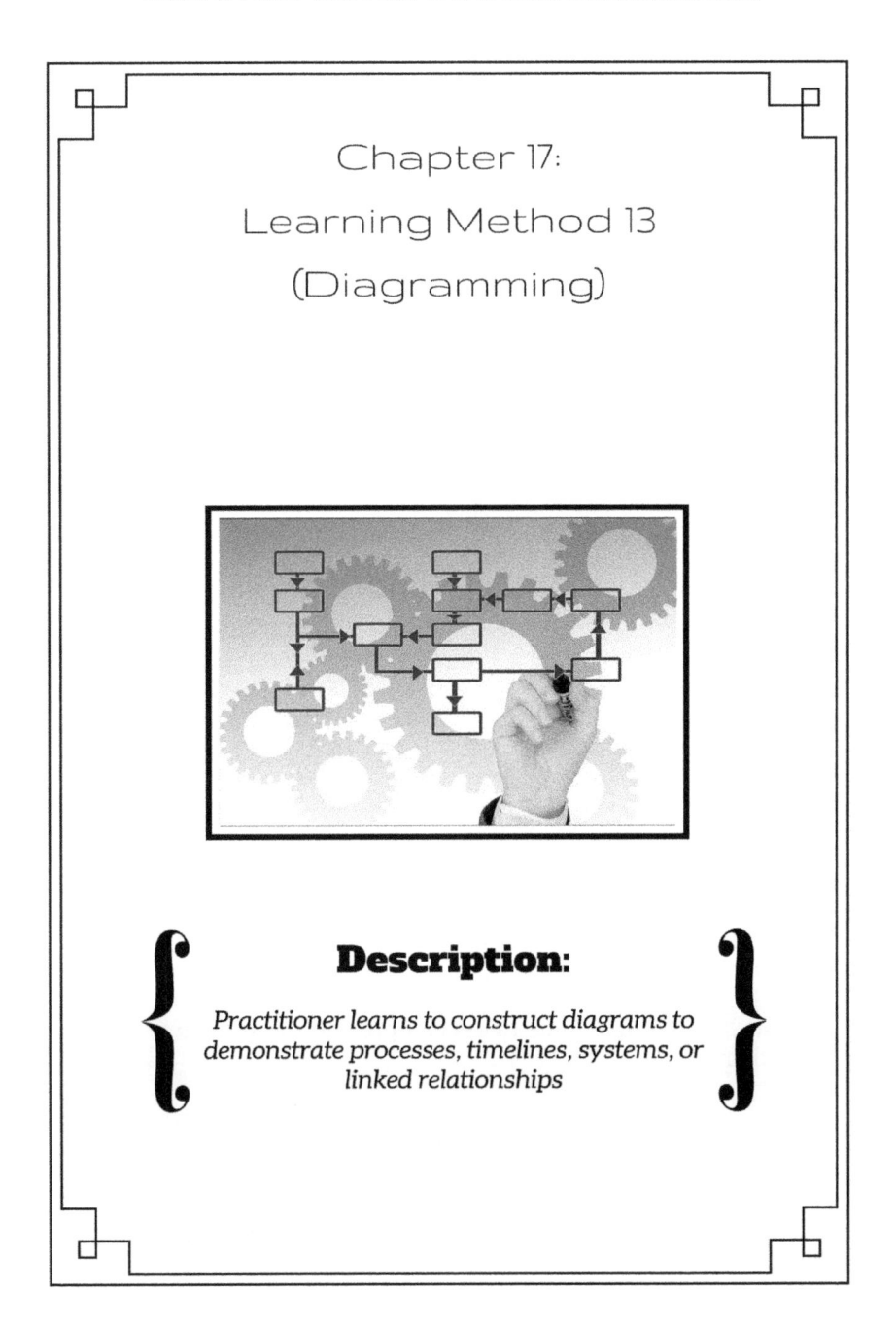

Chapter 17:
Learning Method 13
(Diagramming)

Description:

Practitioner learns to construct diagrams to demonstrate processes, timelines, systems, or linked relationships

The Next Level: SUPERCHARGED

Advantages:

Diagrams allow for visual demonstration of learned knowledge and can add to fast comprehension. Optimal for presentations. Appeals to visual learners and can add value to text based instruction or writing

Disadvantages:

Potential for diagrams to be overly complicated due to creator's knowledge level. Effectiveness of diagram is only as good as the knowledge of the creator. Possibility for inaccuracy or illegibility during creation

Most Likely Practitioners:

Business owners, subject matter experts, presenters, military members, systems engineers, programmers, engineers, business experts, writers, financial analysts, teachers, consultants

Overvew:

Diagramming can be an essential tool for breaking down complex subjects into digestible, easy to process pieces. True practitioners of speed learning and high level educators use diagramming to take something that is verbally difficult to explain and create something that is visually appealing, plus raises comprehension of topic to an audience.

The real value of diagramming is the fact that pictograph and visual instruction can be used to convey knowledge across mixed groups of varying educational levels. There are many forms of diagramming. It is imperative to understand which ones are appropriate for your particular subject.

The Next Level: SUPERCHARGED

Venn Diagrams show where two objects intersect and can be used to isolate which objects fall under two categories

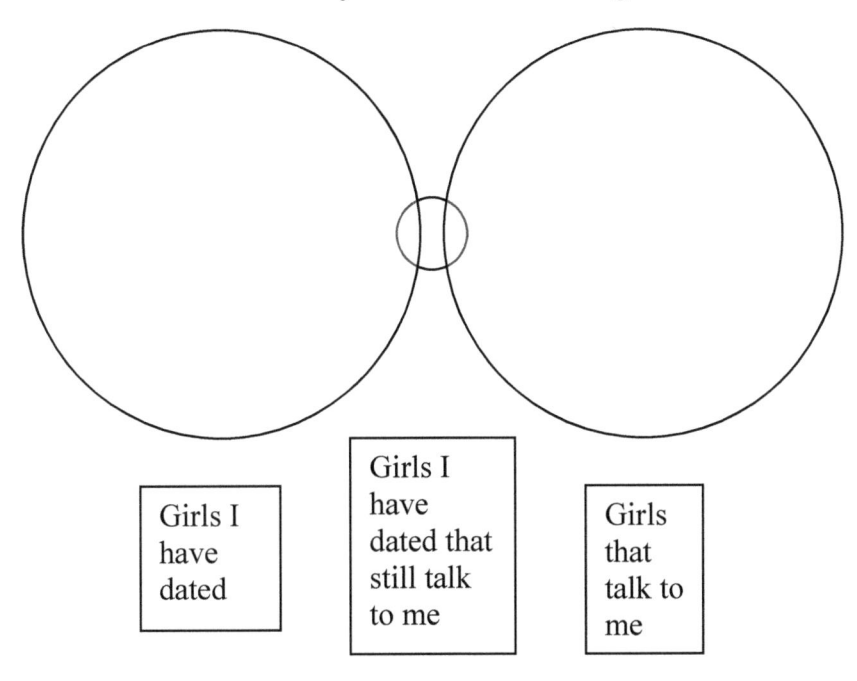

| Girls I have dated | Girls I have dated that still talk to me | Girls that talk to me |

Fig A. Venn Diagram

Flow charts are used to show progression, timelines, or relationships. A vertical flow chart can be used to denote hierarchal structure, military or corporate structure, or leader/subordinate relationships. A horizontal flow chart can denote a progression, timeline, or sequential steps.

College Student ⇒ MBA ⇒ CEO

Fig B. Flow Chart

The Next Level: SUPERCHARGED

Pie charts are used to demonstrate proportion, areas of concern, or to compare numerous data sets in an easy to understand visual construct.

Red = Income from Books
Green = Income from Seminars
Blue = Income from Consulting

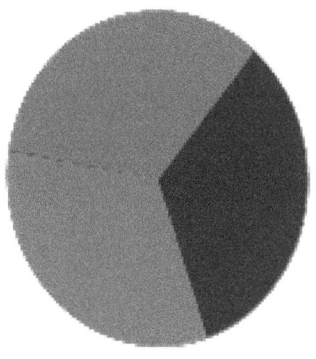

Fig C. Pie Chart

Best Practices:

To properly use diagramming, the user must first ask three things:

1. What is the information that is being converted into a diagram?

*relationship?
*progression?
*goal milestones?
*a complex system?
*components in an engine?
*ingredients in a recipe?
*a hierarchal structure?
*chapters in a book?
*sales goals?
*allotment of student grades?
*a military operation?
*a computer network?

2. Who is the audience that will be receiving and reading this information? (a group of third graders

The Next Level: SUPERCHARGED

3. will be a much different audience than a group of MIT MBAs)

4. What is the complexity level?

Once you have figured out these three questions, you can use diagramming to illustrate your points at a much higher level of confidence.

The Next Level: SUPERCHARGED

The Next Level: SUPERCHARGED

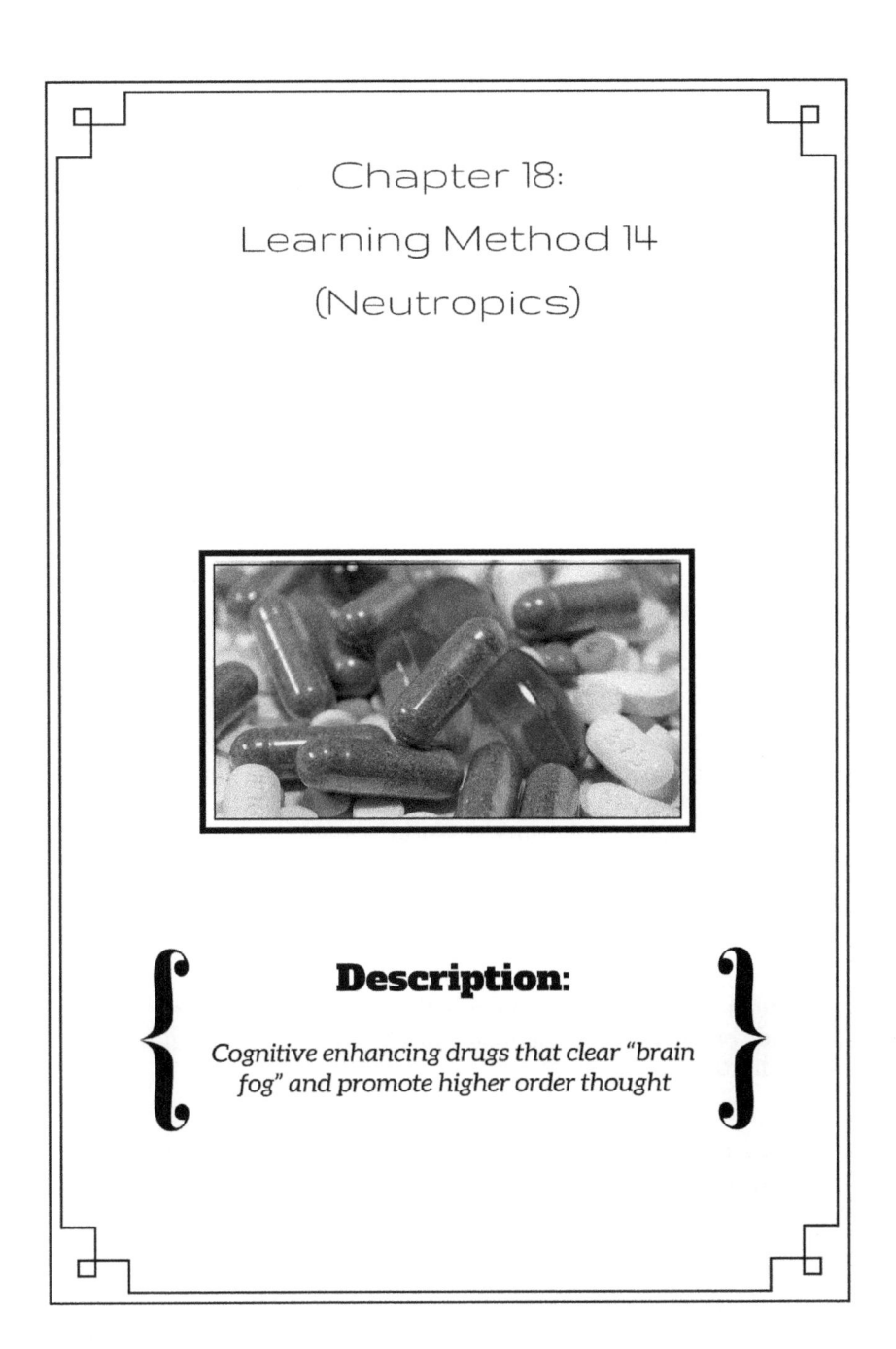

Chapter 18:
Learning Method 14
(Neutropics)

Description:

Cognitive enhancing drugs that clear "brain fog" and promote higher order thought

The Next Level: SUPERCHARGED

Advantages:

Neutropics can create elevated levels of creative thought, can enhance memory recollection and create a higher plane of cognitive understanding of most topics

Disadvantages:

Lack of confirmed scientific studies to support most claims, many scam companies cashing in on low federal regulation

Most Likely Practitioners:

Writers, entrepreneurs, students, business owners, military officers, people in creative industries

Overvew:

Neurotropic drugs are relatively new to the lexicon of cognitive enhancement. The earliest ones that were widely used were in the form of amphetamines given to pilots during long bombing runs in World War 2. These enhancing "superdrugs" kept pilots alert and performing at high levels while flying high-risk dangerous missions.

In 1998, the FDA approved the use of Provigil, an anti-narcoleptic. This and a derivative, Modifinil started to become popular as cognitive enhancers and were allegedly the basis for the fictional drug, NZT, in the movie, "Limitless."

As the desire for mood enhancing and intelligence boosting drugs grew, several companies took the initiative and started focusing on making safer, non-prescription alternatives.
Some of the most popular ones on the market are made from all natural ingredients, have scientific studies on record to

The Next Level: SUPERCHARGED

back up their effectiveness and are available to anyone over 18 without the requirement of a prescription.

Many high level executives and Wall Street/Silicon Valley residents compare neutropic stacks (combos of certain drugs) on threads like Reddit to gain new recipes and formulas. I personally have had amazing results from using Alphabrain and Nootrobox. There is no over-caffeinated feeling that comes with some drugs, and the level at which I am constructing thought is much higher since I started using them.

Best Practices:

In order to maximize the effects of neutropic drugs, I have a morning ritual that "superboosts" the results. If you have the desire to reach a very high level of cognitive thought, try this:

1. Wake up at 5am and take your neutropics (Vitamin B-12/D3/Alphabrain/Rise by Nootrobox/Ginko)
2. Do 15 minutes of hard calisthenic exercises (jumping jacks/pull ups/sit ups/push ups)
3. Take an ice cold shower
4. Walk to a coffee shop at least 8 blocks away
5. Ingest a SMALL amount of caffeine (about 2 shot glasses worth, Americano or Espresso work for me)
6. Walk home and immediately smell scented oil like peppermint

Congratulations, you are now in an OPTIMAL state of mental thought. This is an ideal time to write, construct business plans or to work on new projects.

*I sell both Alphabrain and Nootrobox on my website at www.bluedragonent.com. Click on the "brain drugs" link.

The Next Level: SUPERCHARGED

The Next Level: SUPERCHARGED

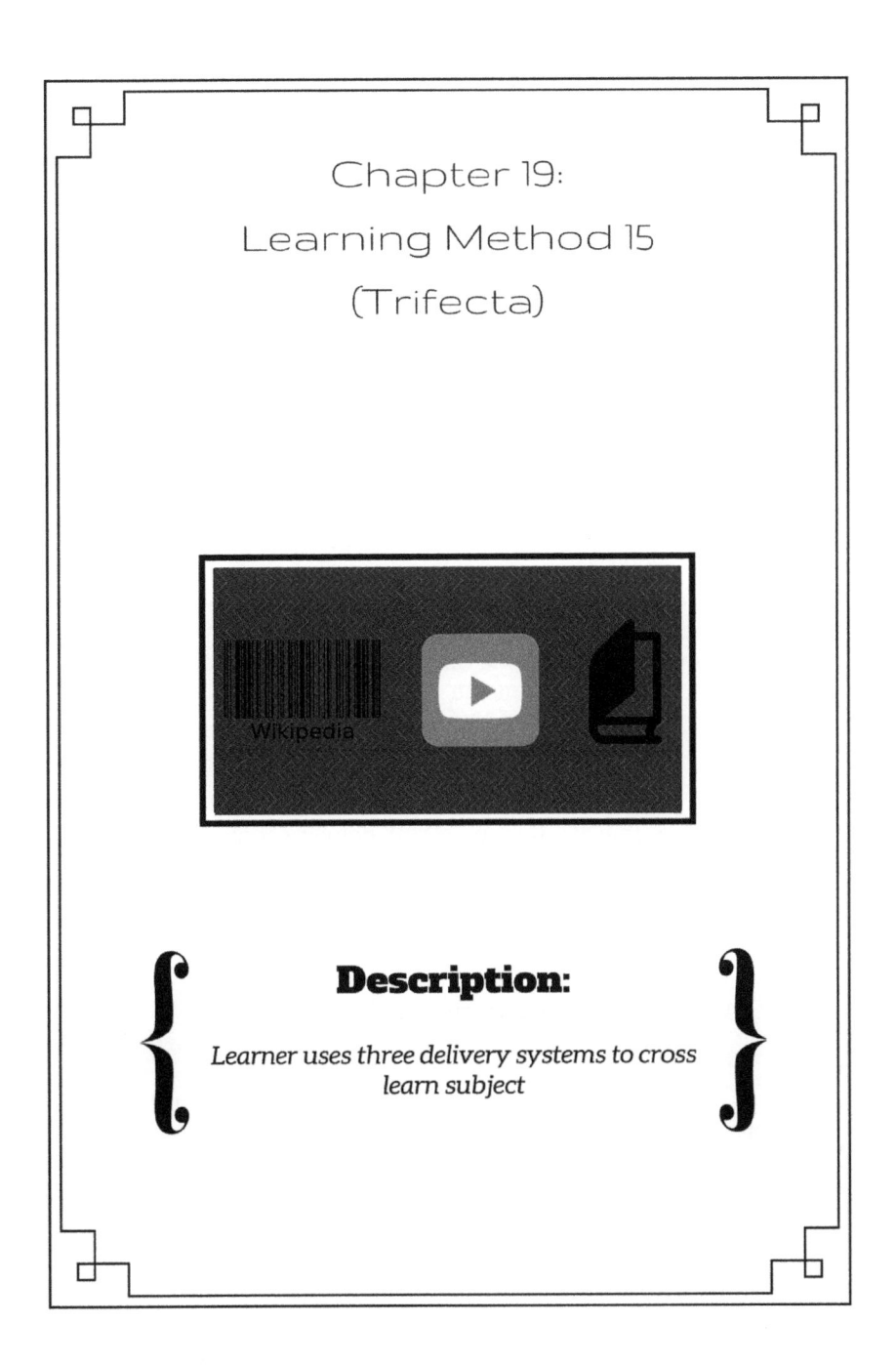

Chapter 19:
Learning Method 15
(Trifecta)

Description:

Learner uses three delivery systems to cross learn subject

The Next Level: SUPERCHARGED

Advantages:

Multi-modal system of delivery
Works well for asymmetrical learners
Far wider exposure to information

Disadvantages:

Time consuming due to more effort involved
Wikipedia not viewed as a "peer reviewed" source in academia

Most Likely Practitioners:

Learners of highly technical or complex subjects
Tactile learners that need to "see it being done"
"Deep processor" learners that need extra information to gain high level comprehension

Overvew:

The Trifecta is a powerful delivery tool for speed learning due to the fact that it incorporates three specific actions:

1. Researching the topic on Wikipedia
2. Watching a Youtube video about the topic
3. Locating the best book written on the topic

By accomplishing these three actions towards a subject, you are leveraging a HUGE fastpass to learning. Once you accomplish the trifecta, a few things will occur:

1. Wikipedia will provide a comprehensive overview, experts in the field, notable events/achievements and a list of peer reviewed sources and articles

The Next Level: SUPERCHARGED

2. A Youtube video will provide auditory and visual instruction usually with voice, text, and musical instruction. This will enhance learning and provide real time examples
3. The best book on a topic will provide expert level knowledge on the subject, usually from a high skill practitioner

Best Practices:

For the Wikipedia section, just do a search for your topic and try a few different word choices to vary the selection. Youtube also has a search engine or you can Google your topic followed by "youtube video" to widen your choices. A book selection needs to be more thorough.

Remember that a book's length doesn't necessarily mean that it has value. Matthew Lesko's stupid book cost me $40 and was worthless. The book I got about Tesla off Amazon was $4 and is only about 35 pages, yet is life changing.

The Next Level: SUPERCHARGED

The Next Level: SUPERCHARGED

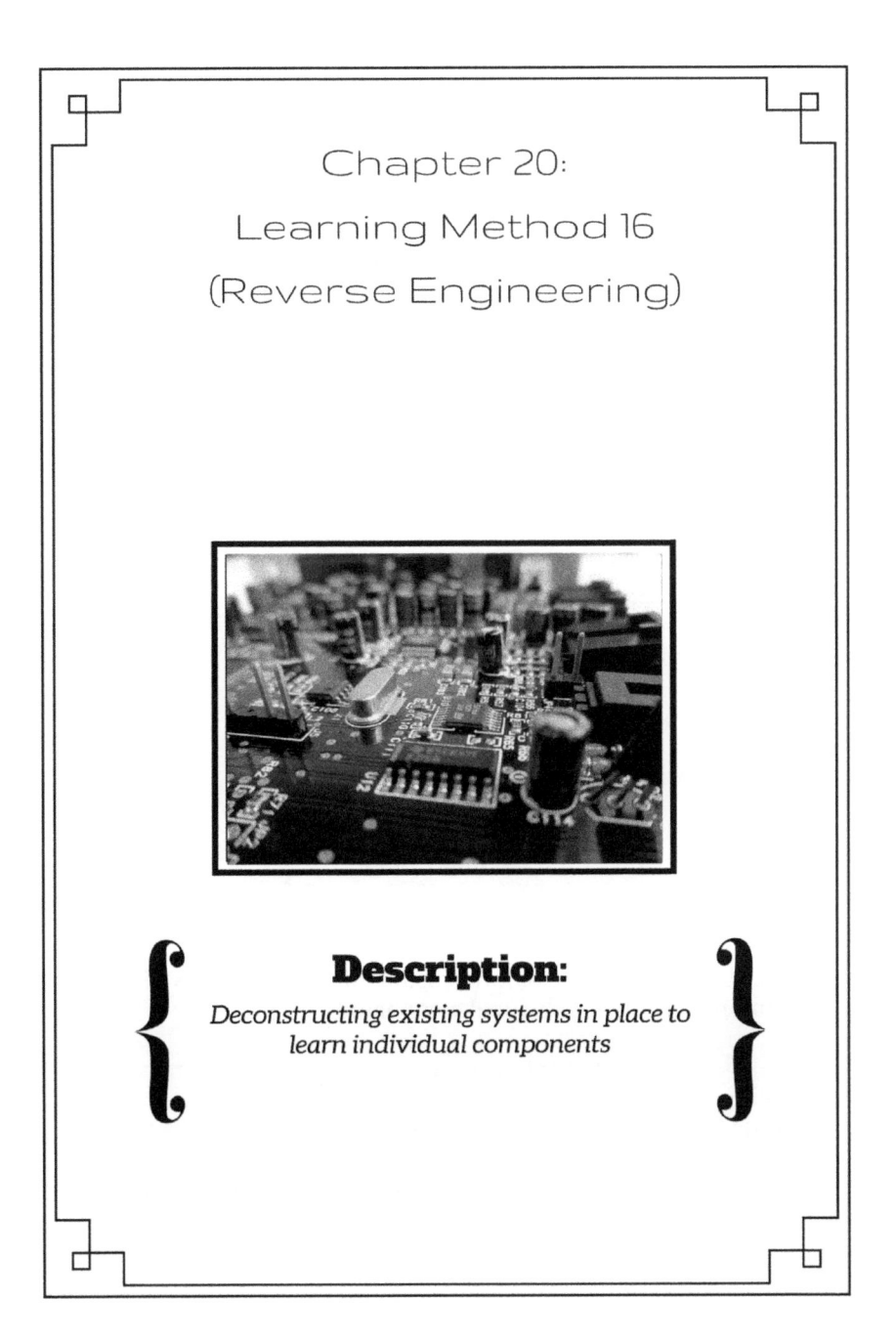

Chapter 20:
Learning Method 16
(Reverse Engineering)

Description:
Deconstructing existing systems in place to learn individual components

The Next Level: SUPERCHARGED

Advantages:

Learner gains wider understanding of both parts and whole system
Gives several examples of systems vs just one
Can show learner elements that would normally be hidden

Disadvantages:

Requires attention to detail
Can constitute plagiarism if not done properly
Requires longer amount of time to properly detail pieces of system
Ineffective for single component systems

Most Likely Practitioners:

Web designers
Writers
Creators
Inventors
Learners with high levels of spatial reasoning

Overvew:

Reverse engineering is a basic concept, yet is challenging to implement properly. It involves attention to detail, observation, comprehension of systems as well as comprehension of individual components.

The real advantage to reverse engineering is that you will be able to see how something is constructed and can use those ideas to strengthen *your* project or creation. It is vital to note that reverse engineering does not give you the right to steal, plagiarize, copy, or appropriate someone's hard work.

The Next Level: SUPERCHARGED

It DOES, however, give you the ability to separate individual components, isolate their function, and usability, and then create something completely original or vastly improve what you already have.

Here is the difference. For my life coaching website, www.bluedragonent.com, I needed some ideas because I didn't know what a life coaching site should have.

I Googled five life coaching sites and started taking notes. Here is the difference between copying someone and doing reverse engineering:

Copying:

1. Using exact links/fonts/patterns/words
2. Placing pictures exactly in same area on page
3. Having EXACT format and spacing

Reverse Engineering:

1. Noting general guidelines (smaller links at top/"as seen on")
2. Paying attention to types of coaching pictures (group shots/headshots/abstract objects?)
3. Noting features such as online store, t shirt sales, DVD sets...etc

Best Practices:

Find 3-5 high quality sources to reverse engineer. Get out paper and start writing down observations. What do you see that looks amazing? How are components linked? What is the functionality? What works well with YOUR project or creation? What are they doing that you are not?

Could you do something similar without copying them? Start listing descriptions,

The Next Level: SUPERCHARGED

features, components used and also implement Next Level technique, "Diagramming" to sketch how everything is linked together.

> Dr. Rob's notes:
> Reverse engineering is great for websites, book design, electronic configuration, clothing styles, business platforms and system design

The Next Level: SUPERCHARGED

Chapter 21:

The Next Level:

HOLLYWOOD

The Next Level: SUPERCHARGED

Chapter 21: Next Level: Hollywood

Despite Hollywood's best attempts at dumbing the populace down with spoiled celebutantes on reality TV, action movies that fill us with car chases and violence, and endless commercials, there are some glimmering diamonds in the cultural coal mine known as popular culture.

I have selected a few television shows and movies that eschew Next Level concepts and give a good representation of what higher intelligence looks like.

The reader that seeks the Next Level would be wise to gather inspiration from Hollywood's interpretation of higher intellect and the habits employed by these high IQ wonders.

Movies

Limitless- Bradley Cooper is Eddie Moura, a down on his luck writer. His girlfriend leaves him, his rent is due, and his novel has gone nowhere. A chance occurrence gives him the ability to try a pill that gives him a four digit IQ. He begins speaking other languages, reading voraciously, gets a great job as a business analyst, and finishes his novel in four days.

Next Level concepts- Moura uses Learning Method 1: Research, to aid him in his endeavors. He reads copious amounts of business reports to learn about competitors and looks up company information while doing research for stock market investment.

Phenomenon- John Travolta is George Malley, a mechanic in a small town in central California. One night a flash of light hits him and he begins accruing intelligence rapidly. He speaks multiple languages, reads hundreds of books, and helps improve the lives of everyone around him.

The Next Level: SUPERCHARGED

Next Level concepts- Malley also uses Learning Method 1: Research, to help him in his projects. He reads books about a wide variety of subjects including biology and science. He incorporates Learning Method 7: Creation, when he builds a car that gets 70 miles per gallon running off pig manure. The running theme of the movie is Research Method 3: Tutelage. Malley has a close mentor in the towns doctor, played by Robert
Duvall, who guides George and provides his advice for George's new found powers and intellect.

Good Will Hunting- Matt Damon is genius Will Hunting, a Boston janitor with a propensity for criminal behavior. Throughout the movie, he displays genius traits and behavior, from debating a Harvard graduate student and winning, to solving a friend's organic chemistry homework with ease.

Next Level concepts- Will is reading throughout the movie, therefore using Learning Method 1: Research, to better his understanding of history, math, law, and mathematics. He starts attending court ordered sessions with his therapist, played by Robin Williams. Their relationship illustrates the value of Learning Method 3: Tutelage. Will begins receiving life advice and guidance in using his intellect for the betterment of his life.

Television

Sherlock- Based on the works of Sir Arthur Conan Doyle, Sherlock is based in modern day England. Sherlock, aided by his assistant, Dr. Watson, solve difficult crimes by using Sherlock's amazing propensity for logical deduction and observation.

The Next Level: SUPERCHARGED

Next Level concepts- Sherlock does a high amount of internet exploration in order to gather his large body of intellectual knowledge on obscure subjects. This entails Learning Method 1: Research. Holmes also illustrates Learning Method 9: Immersion, by employing disguises and blending in with the local populace to gather information. He does not simply dabble in detective work, he *lives* it by directly inserting himself in the world of the case he is currently investigating.

House MD- Gregory House is one of New Jersey's most highly regarded diagnostic medical specialists. Employing a team of junior doctors, House races against time in order to save his patients' lives.

Next Level concepts- House employs several Learning Methods to accomplish his high degree of medical success. He attended a prestigious medical school, therefore, using Learning Concept 5: Formal Education. He employs Learning Concept 8: Socratic Method, when holding diagnostic meetings with his team in order to draw out a higher body of knowledge.

The habits that all of these characters use can help you in pursuit of your own growth. A summative review shows that they engage in the following:

*Read a variety of information from several sources
*Use people as a source of information
*Ask high end questions in order to increase comprehension
*Observe a far higher amount than their contemporaries
*Engage in regular exercise to further stimulate the mind

Maybe Hollywood does have some value, after all.

The Next Level: SUPERCHARGED

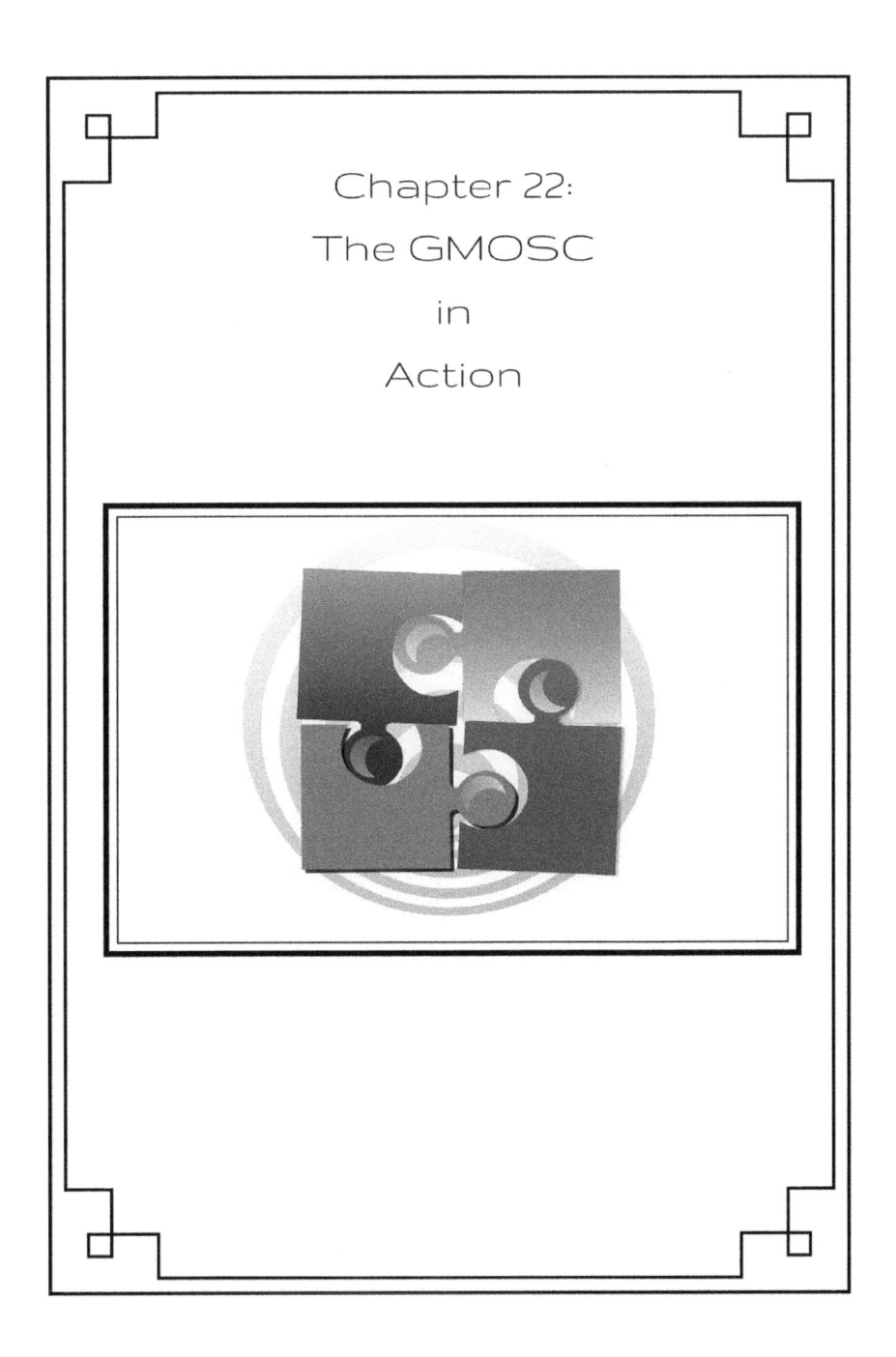

Chapter 22: The GMOSC in Action

The Next Level: SUPERCHARGED

By now, you should be excited. You have read about self education, have probably thought of something you wanted to get better at, and maybe even used the GMOSC to get a mental estimate of self assessment. You have been shown ten great ways to get better at your career or skill. For the final pages of this book, I wanted to demonstrate how people of different backgrounds could use this book to maximize their growth.

I will present you with three fictional people that use the GMOSC and Learning Methods to advance in their personal growth. By reading about their application of the concepts presented, you'll gather the best possible ways to use this book.

Next Level Candidate 1
Cindy
Age: 16
Skill/Career to be improved: Owning own company
Current GMOSC rating: Awareness

Cindy is a regular teenager, she goes to school, talks with her friends on Facebook, and listens to OneDirection. After reading about several teens in Fast Company Magazine that started their own companies, she was hooked and wanted to start her own clothing company for teen girls.

Using the GMOSC, she realized that she only knew the bare minimums of clothing design, sales, marketing, and website development. She read the Next Level and found three methods that were most tailored to her life: Research (she loved to read), Tutelage (her aunt owned a boutique out of town), and Creation (she knew how to sew clothing from her sewing class at school).

Cindy immediately set up a multi-tiered plan using the Next Level concepts. Despite being 16, she used the resources available to her and was able to overcome her obstacles.

The Next Level: SUPERCHARGED

Cindy would then accomplish the following steps:

1. Made weekly phone calls to her aunt to learn the nuances of pricing, website development, seasonal inventories, and basic retail theory (Tutelage).
2. Cindy looked up other teen clothing designers online and read about how they created their fashion lines. She then ordered a book about creating and marketing clothing from Amazon (Research).
3. Cindy devoted a few weekends and part of summer break to create five sample items immediately. She knew that in order to be taken seriously at department stores, she would need examples of her work (Creation).

Cindy's company utilizes social media and is a hit. She makes enough to afford Fashion School and her clothing line inspires many other young girls to start their own companies.

The Next Level: SUPERCHARGED

Next Level Candidate 2
Jose
Age: 42
Skill/Career to be improved: Sales
Current GMOSC rating: Proficient

Jose is 42, with a family. He has taken a new job at a luxury car lot and because of the holiday season, has been told that he should start after the new year. He has previous experience in sales and has a few classes in Psychology under his belt.

Using the GMOSC, Jose realizes that he is confident in sales and experienced. He rates himself Proficient and chooses three methodologies that fit his lifestyle and resources. He realizes that he is eager to get back into the sales game so he plans on starting immediately (Immersion). He then realizes that he wants to follow the best so he decides to learn the methods and tactics of famous people that excelled in human relations and sales tactics (Emulation + Research).

Jose would then do the following steps:

1. Calls his future employer and offers to work one day for free if they bring him on immediately
2. (Immersion). His boss would be very foolish to turn this down.
3. Does a Google search (Research) on some of the best salespeople in the world. Orders materials from Zig Ziglar and Win Friends and Influence People by Dale Carnegie (Emulation).

Within a year, Jose is Sales Manager.

The Next Level: SUPERCHARGED

Next Level Candidate 3
Keisha
Age: 23
Skill/Career to be improved: Food Distribution and Sales
Current GMOSC rating: Familiar

Keisha is a recent college grad with a degree in Business. For her Senior year in college, she came up with the idea of selling food based on her grandmother's recipes. She has no idea how to start a restaurant, much less get the funding for it.

Keisha used the GMOSC to self assess at a level of Familiar. She decided that the methods that would best suit her goals would be to find someone that opened a small, minority owned restaurant (Emulation), learn about venture funding (Research), and find a mentor (Tutelage).

She made a multi-tiered business plan that involved the following:

1. Google searched several women owned diners and restaurants in her town. Looked up venture capital events nearby (Research).
2. Looked up women owned restaurants nationwide and started annotating actionable tasks for her own plan (Emulation).
3. Called several restaurants and conducted telephone interviews until she found an owner that could monitor her progress and offer guidance (Tutelage).

The Next Level: SUPERCHARGED

The Next Level: SUPERCHARGED

Chapter 23:

Real Life Examples

The Next Level: SUPERCHARGED

The Next Level: SUPERCHARGED

"The Runners"

Dick and Richard Hoyt

Next Level Methodology:
Emotional Connection

Accomplishment:
Finishing over a thousand endurance events together with one member diagnosed with cerebral palsy.

The Next Level: SUPERCHARGED

RG: *Dick, thank you for this interview. When you first decided that you were going to compete in events with your son, what physical shape were you in?*

DH: I was 15 lbs. overweight and not in very good shape. I was in the military full time and had my own masonry business, which helped me from putting on too much additional weight.

RG: *How did you prepare for that first event mentally and physically?*

DH: I just made up my mind mentally that we would run and finish the 5 mile race. It was not easy but we did finish coming in next to last. I had to keep focused an keep telling myself that we could do it. I could not walk for 2 weeks after the race and every muscle in mind body was aching and sore.

RG: *At that very first event, was there a fear of letting your son down if you didn't perform at the expected level?*

DH: There was no fear of letting Rick down as I had a very positive attitude that we would finish the race. And if Rick

The Next Level: SUPERCHARGED

enjoyed the race I would train and get myself in shape so that we would be able to take part in other race events.

RG: *After your first event, did it change your opinion of your own physical capabilities? Did you have the moment of, "I can do a lot more than I had realized."*

DH: It was after our 2nd race that changed my opinion of my physical capabilities, as we finished 150th out of 300 runners-some who were quite fast, and I realized that we were going to be able to be competitive with these other runners. And this was only after training for a few months, so I knew if I continued training I would be in even better shape.

RG: *This book, The Next Level, is about raising the level of performance at a skill or career. How many races/events did Team Hoyt participate in before a self realization of your increased capabilities took place?*

DH: Our Next Level came when we decided to run in our first Boston Marathon. We had completed 15 races up until then, with the longest distance being an 18.6 mile race. So I knew I was going to have to set up the training for this event of 26.2 miles.

RG: *After awhile, running wasn't enough. Team Hoyt raised the bar yet again by incorporating bicycling and swimming. What brought on this drastic increase in difficulty for the events?*

DH: Dave McGillivary (race director of the Boston Marathon and Falmouth, MA Road Race) saw us running the Falmouth Road Race in 1984 and came up to me and said I looked like I would be a good triathlete. We were able to get some equipment made; I learned how to swim and got back on a bike (which I had not been on since I was 6 years old) and upped my training routines, and we took part in our first triathlon on Father's Day

The Next Level: SUPERCHARGED

in 1985. It was a 1 mile swim, 40 mile bike ride and a 10 mile run.

RG: *Rick increased his own capabilities by finishing college. What advice would Team Hoyt give to other people with disabilities about goal setting?*

DH: Goal setting is very important to achieve success. We struggled to get Rick mainstreamed into public school, and then into local high school and then Boston University. We kept having the doors closed in our face, but we persevered and never gave up until we achieved our goal. After we started running we set up a goal to run and bike across the UA from CA to Boston, which we did in 1992.

RG: *When I was outlining the chapters for this book, you were my first choice for the section entitled, "Emotional Connection." Can you describe the effect that the love for your son had on your decision to compete in events together?*

DH: When Rick and I started competing in races and triathlons together, it really bonded us together emotionally. We were working together for a common goal of crossing the finish line- he with his heart and soul and me with my arms and legs. It needs the 2 of us together to do this- we cannot do it without each other to get us over the line. I felt the connection with Rick every time we start a race, and it continues through the race until we cross the line. We work as a team for one common goal.

RG: *Thank you for your service, what advice would you have for our military readers that need that extra push to achieve their goals?*

DH: The Team Hoyt Motto is "Yes You Can" – there is no such word as "can't" in the Hoyt vocabulary. Being in the military is very stressful on the enlisted person and their family and everyday issues are added to when the enlisted person is away from home for several months at a time. You just have to remember to set personal goals for yourself, and

The Next Level: SUPERCHARGED

always do your best to try to work to achieve these goals. You will feel better about yourself with each goal you achieve.

RG: *Achieving goals that have a personal or emotional connection involved is much harder because of the fear of failure. Can you share a time when you may have hit your physical wall, and used your son to mentally push yourself even further?*

DH: Rick is the one who inspires and motivates me so because of him I usually do not hit a wall. The only time I can remember hitting the wall was at mile 22 of our first Boston Marathon. I was drained and was not sure if I could go on, so I walked for a little ways, and then Rick started making noises and moving his arms to say "it's ok Dad- we got this". I got a spurt of energy and because of his encouragement I was able to go on to push him across the finish line.

RG: *Thank you Dick, it's been an honor. Please give my regards to Rick. My readers are very lucky to read about your story together.*

The Next Level: SUPERCHARGED

The Next Level: SUPERCHARGED

"The Fitness Magnate"

Katrina Lucero

Next Level Methodology: Creation

Accomplishment: Created first online magazine focused on fitness competitors that have tattoos/body modifications: "Fitness Inked"

The Next Level: SUPERCHARGED

RG: *Katrina, can you describe the events in your life that steered you towards adopting a life based on fitness principles?*

I was always in sports, never voluntarily. I joined the Army in 2005 and sustained an injury during a training exercise. Due to the injury, I gained close to 90 pounds. Three herniated discs in my back made any impact activity painful, difficult, and uncomfortable enough that I just wasn't interested.

The Army gave me two options to fix my back pain; they could fuse my spine or do a gastric bypass. I opted to have a bypass in 2010. The pre-requisites for the surgery included losing 15% of the excess body weight I carried. I got a personal trainer, changed my eating habits, and buckled down.

After the surgery, I stayed on with the trainer and lost an additional 90 pounds. All told, my weight of 275 at my heaviest stays around a comfortable and fit 155 now.

RG: *After the weight loss, what made you want to dive into a completely uncharted territory (tattooed fitness) and create the website?*

Though I wouldn't consider myself artistic, I always appreciated the art that people displayed, with their bodies as the canvas. I had gotten three small tattoos while I was in the Army, each of which had ties to my culture and heritage.

I gave myself a goal of becoming a fitness model. Getting paid to work out was my idea of heaven!

Once I had lost weight and began toning, I started participating in photo shoots. I was told that it was a futile effort, that women with tattoos wouldn't be sponsored for national advertisements.

I was PISSED!

I started the site to prove that it could, in fact, be done.

RG: *Were people negative initially?*

The Next Level: SUPERCHARGED

I wouldn't say they had negative reactions. Most of them were mildly supportive, more were confused.

RG: *Once the website started catching on, can you describe how you reinvented yourself and the steps you took to become a businesswoman in this field with no experience, no education, and no one helping you?*

It's been a case of trial and error the whole way. What doesn't work gets revamped, reworked, and tried again.

RG: *What are some of the criticisms that were directed towards you?*

That this combination, tattoos and fitness, was too niche.
This combination made no sense.
It would never catch on.

RG: *What does the Katrina of today do business-wise, that the Katrina of a year ago didn't?*

Going ahead full steam. No more tenuous, half-assing. Just diving in.

RG: *You literally went from the bottom step on the GMOSC model (awareness) to the middle (proficient) in about a year and a half, which is remarkable. What habits or attributes do you credit for this remarkable jump?*

Motivation, mostly. I know where I WANT to be. I just am trying every avenue to GET there.

RG: *What advice would you give to young people that want to start their own business ventures but are scared of being laughed at?*

It doesn't matter if you're laughed at. Being secure in yourself will free you from caring what other people think. Once that doesn't matter, you can do ANYTHING

The Next Level: SUPERCHARGED

RG: *What are the fastest steps they could use to succeed?*

KNOW YOURSELF!
Pursue what you're passionate about, but don't be stubborn about the path to get there.
Be open to criticism and know how to discern critiques from "hatin'".

RG: What's in the future for Fitness Inked?
Apparel, merchandise, print edition of the magazine and global domination.

The Next Level: SUPERCHARGED

"The Skateboarder"

Frankie Hill

Next Level Methodology: Immersion

Accomplishment: First skateboarder to consistently skate large handrails/large gaps

The Next Level: SUPERCHARGED

RG: *Frankie, thanks for the interview. This book, The Next Level, is about teaching people to rapidly advance their abilities at a skill or their career. What got you into skateboarding?*

FH: What got me in was hanging out with my friend. He had a skateboard and I was on a bike. I saw him ollie off a street transition and he got higher than I did on a bike. I knew at that moment I wanted to skateboard. It seemed very free to have a small board under you that you could control rather than a large bike.

RG: *You and I had a conversation once about both of us using skateboarding as a distraction from a sketchy home life. What motivated you to skate so hard and to give so much?*

FH: I always found it fun and just trying to learn new tricks was what pushed me. Getting away from home was a very important part of that. I definitely enjoyed getting out of the house and learning to skateboard. It was my chance to be free and to be on my own. I definitely enjoyed getting out of the house and learning how to skateboard.

RG: *Can you tell us about your injuries you received while in your Powell days?*

FH: I was skating at the Powell facility and was done for the day. I had skated for 5-6 hours and a well known photographer showed up when I was walking out and talked me into going to UCSB and talked me into skating for a poster book for Transworld. I did a backside lipslide down a handrail and felt good about it. I wanted a backup picture and I ollied a wall and fully extended my foot. I had to push myself home on my skateboard. When I got home, there was a message saying that they were pulling my Transworld poster and giving it to Adam Mcnatt. He got a frontside nosegrind.

The Next Level: SUPERCHARGED

RG: *I know you don't like praise or accolades; in fact you're one of the most humble guys I've ever met. What did you do to get so damn good between Public Domain and Ban This? There are tricks in Ban This that had NEVER been done before.*

FH: I believe I learned from other skaters and by the time I had gotten to Public Domain, my skateboarding had developed from the point of what I learned and I was able to put my own spin on it. I learned from Ray Barbee, Tommy Guerrerro, Tim Jackson from Dogtown, of course Mike Vallely. I was able to take the tricks I had learned and was able to add to them from the skaters around me.

RG: *One of the things that really made you stand out was the fact that you combined your aggressive skating style with newer tricks in 92 like the late shove it and the pressure flip. Did you have any trouble going from one style of skating to literally creating your own?*

FH: I have always felt it was fun to do little flatground tricks and technical tricks. I had a little more time to learn those in the 92 time. I may have invented the pressure flip, I'm not sure. I made up the kick frigid fingerflip. Powell had me in the Public Domain slam section but I had made it. After I made that I wanted to take those tricks and do it down something big. Like the 360 double flip down five stairs.

The Next Level: SUPERCHARGED

RG: *You still have one of the best Japan (mute) grabs ever. Do you think that certain tricks will always be in style?*

FH: I'm not sure. I think skateboarding has developed and changed quite a bit. I don't know if grabs will always be around. I think the grabs may fade out, but I hope they are something that will be around. Its just one more different style you can add to your skateboarding. They add style. I definitely believe that grabbing your skateboard can add style. The one thing I loved about street skating is the originality. The different tricks. Not everyone doing the same tricks is what I love about it. If everyone does the same thing, it seems to be very boring if you ask me.

RG: *What would you say to that little kid that is just starting skating and wants to be pro? What advice would you give him?*

FH: I would tell him that basically you have to be an optimist. That every time you try a trick that you will land it. If you don't land it, it will be the next time. You

The Next Level: SUPERCHARGED

have to keep hope alive. You know its a good sign when the filmer goes home and leaves you there. If you've got the drive to continue on no matter what, that's what its going to take to succeed. That actually goes for anything in this world. You cant walk away and you cant accept failure at any cost.

RG: *In 1990, I was 14, living with my hoarder grandmother, and almost all my relatives were on drugs. It was the worst time I ever got through. All I had was my Bones sweats and Ban This. I thought about killing myself all the time. I HATED my life. You got me through that by showing me how awesome skating could be. What advice would you give to kids that look up to you that might not have the best home life?*

FH: I would tell a kid that their greatest asset is themself. You cant look to anybody else to help you out in life. Don't look to other people for their enjoyment and personal satisfaction in this world. You cant be negative, you have to be an optimist. You just gotta fight. Every day is a fight when you wake up. As long as you put yourself first and don't let negative influences get to you, you have a good chance of creating positive feelings for yourself in this world.

RG: *Who do you look up to?*

FH: I look up to anyone that has an opinion that they can stand behind it. Even if its the wrong opinion. At least they have one. I can respect someone like that. They are easy to find. When you're talking to someone and they have no real point of view on anything are just there, those are the people I don't respect. You have to have your own point of view and you have to be motivated in this world to get anywhere. That also adds to the originality of this world. So I respect anybody that is motivated in this world, to be honest.

The Next Level: SUPERCHARGED

RG: *What does the future hold skating wise, for Frankie Hill?*

FH: I don't know what skateboarding holds for me in the future. Its given me everything I have always wanted in this world. Its given me hope, its given me a place to go, its given me a place to get away, if something came up for me, Id be grateful of course. Its given me everything I have ever wanted. That's the beautiful thing about skateboarding. You just never know what is around the next coroner as long as you stay positive and keep the hope along inside you, there's always a better day tomorrow, you just have to know you are going to have to fight for it.

The Next Level: SUPERCHARGED

"The US Army Ranger"

Joseph Kapacziewski

Next Level Methodology: Emotional Connection

Accomplishment: First soldier to be reinstated to full active duty combat status with a prosthetic limb.

The Next Level: SUPERCHARGED

RG: *Joe, you've had an amazing life. What fuels that unstoppable drive of yours?*

JK: As a child, my father instilled a work ethic in me to always try your hardest and always strive to be the best that you can be. My accident did not steer me from this moral standard that I have had since childhood. I constantly feel the need to prove myself and prove that my accident did not make me any less capable than an able bodied person.

RG: *You decided early on that you would only be the best once you enlisted in the Army. Did you have negative people in your life that tried to talk you out of it? How did you deal with them?*

JK: I had some people who worried about me and knew the potential hazards of being in the military. My family has always felt concerned but they never told me "absolutely do not do this".
I don't have time in my life for negative people. I try to steer clear of negativity and make the nest choices that I can.

RG: *You're literally the Army's top 1%. What habits or behaviors did you adopt to reach your levels of performance?*

JK: I have a "never quit" attitude and a mentality that someone has done this before me so there is no reason that I cannot achieve anything that I am tasked with.

RG: *For our civilian readers, Ranger School is three months of sleep deprivation, starvation, and the expectation of candidates to make good leadership decisions while learning assault tactics, mountaineering, parachuting, and firearm proficiency. Was there a part of Ranger school that was tough for your to learn? How did you get past the most difficult times?*

JK: The toughest part of RS for me was food deprivation because I am a fat kid at heart. Sleep deprivation was also extremely tough to get used to because you want to make the

The Next Level: SUPERCHARGED

right and best decision for the men that you are leading but sleep deprivation clouds your thinking and judgment.

RG: *Joe, the fact that you were skilled enough to get a Ranger Tab and Scroll is impressive, but after you were wounded, you had to get requalified with a prosthetic leg. How did you mentally and physically prepare yourself for such a daunting task?*

JK: I really had to approach it one day at a time. I set a long term goal of being able to pass all of the Ranger standards and I set a string of short term goals that set me up for success to accomplish those long term goals of requalifying. With the right mindset, I think you can accomplish anything mentally or physically.

RG: *What's your take on confidence vs. arrogance? You've achieved because of a "door kicker" attitude towards your goals. How do you know when to draw the line?*

JK: Confidence is knowing through experiences that you can do something. Arrogance to me is sort of bragging about your accomplishments. You need to be a confident leader but growing up in the Ranger Rgmt, you realize there is no room for arrogance because there is always someone who is faster, stronger and can shoot better than you.

The Next Level: SUPERCHARGED

RG: *For the high school students reading this that are military bound, how would Sgt. Kap advise them to be top performers?*

JK: Be physically fit. Being in shape is a personal choice. Pounding pavement, doing pushups and pull-ups are free - it just takes time and effort to be really good at them. Service members that are physically fit are usually noticed and stand out among their peers. It takes discipline to accomplish being physically fit and this trait typically helps a person to be a leader.

RG: *You've literally created new DOD policy for wounded vets by "leading the way." What three pieces of advice would you give to these veterans that are coping with injuries and trying to adapt to a new chapter in their life?*

The Next Level: SUPERCHARGED

JK: 1. Surround yourself with positive people
2. Set short and long term goals on what you want to accomplish
3. Realize that nothing in this world is free or easy. It is going to take a great deal of hard work and effort to accomplish your goals and reach your potential.

RG: *How can the military better help wounded veterans?*

JK: From my experiences, the military has put many programs in place to help our wounded veterans. Some of them are not easy to navigate but if you are proactive, you will be able to get the services that you need.

RG: *What are Sgt. Kap's goals for the next five years?*

JK: MILLION DOLLAR QUESTION! - haha
Continue to serve my country, spend time with my family and try to help motivate wounded soldiers.

The Next Level: SUPERCHARGED

The Next Level: SUPERCHARGED

"Entrepreneurial Network Titans"

Josh and Jill Stanton

Next Level Methodology:
Networking/Mastermind
Creation
Immersion

Accomplishment:
Achieved Sustainable Financial Freedom
Through Subscriber-Based Entrepreneurial
Network

The Next Level: SUPERCHARGED

Josh and Jill Stanton are the co-founders of Screw the Nine to Five—a little slice of the internet where that helps entrepreneurs take their already-existing businesses to the next level.

They've been featured by entrepreneurial heavyweights such as John Lee Dumas, Amy Porterfield and Chris Ducker and have graced the pages of The Huffington Post, Under 30 CEO and Laura Roeder.

They have created a hyper-supportive community and have a monthly membership community (Screw U) that teaches budding (and more seasoned) entrepreneurs how to create and grow online businesses that light them up.

Their infamous Screw the Nine to Five Community Facebook group is filled with insightful, positive and supportive entrepreneurs (who refer to themselves as "Scroupies") that encourage each other with an almost cult-like zeal.

RG: Think back to when you were working a 9-to-5...what did you hate about it?

JS: For me it was being told what to do.

Honestly, I am the world's worst employee and hate being told what to do, how to do it and when to do it.

Josh, however, hated the lack of time freedom.

He loves nothing more than to create his day how he wants and spend his time on projects he truly enjoys.

RG: Did you feel like you were working under your potential?

JS: 100%. I hated nothing more than going into work and "punching a clock" and each time I did it, I felt like a little part of me died.

The Next Level: SUPERCHARGED

The worst part was, I didn't know what to do about it and it wasn't until a few years had past (and I met Josh) that I finally hit my breaking point and got serious about creating a business online.

RG: Did you have an exact point where you hated your jobs so much that you decided to set out on your own?

JS: Josh was pretty early on. He was out by the time he was 21, after sticking it out in an internship for 18 months.

I on the other hand took a bit longer.

While I knew I wanted to start a business (and tried 3 different times from the age of 25), it wasn't until I turned 29 that I finally started a business that worked.

And not just worked, but made money and was profitable...a.k.a the sweetest feeling in the world!

RG: When you guys started planning this venture, did you catch any grief from friends and family?

JS: Yes and no...

I mean, in the beginning we got a LOT of blank looks and comments like "are you still working? I thought you worked for yourself?" or my favourite "what will you do if this little business doesn't work out?".

But now? Now that we've been at it for years and we're self sufficient and our business has really hit its stride those comments are less common. However, we still get a few blank stares when we go on a tear about business. *wink*

RG: At what point did you guys know that this was sustainable, and that you had finally made it?

The Next Level: SUPERCHARGED

JS: I mean, I always knew that we would make it work. There was never a doubt in my mind about that because I believe Screw the Nine to Five is a movement.

It's bigger than just "online business training"...it's more of a way of life.

So I never *really* worried if it would work, I always just I *felt* that it would.

However, with that being said, it was only around mid-June once we switched to a monthly membership model (recurring revenue) that we really starting seeing the predictable income and the opportunities that come with that.

Have we "made it" though?

I think we still have some work to do to get to that point.

RG: What are a few mistakes entrepreneurs make in the first few years?

JS: The biggest one I see happening is they give up too soon.

They think that just because they've put in a year of hard work and they don't have tons of money to show for it that it's "not working", when really they are closer than they've ever been.

Lack of patience is a huge issue I see quite often.

That and the fear of failure.

RG: Do you think everyone should try and start their own business?

JS: No, I don't actually.

The Next Level: SUPERCHARGED

And I know that sounds weird, but I truly believe that ANYONE can be an entrepreneur, but not everyone can do it.

What I mean is we entrepreneurs are a special breed. We're more comfortable with risk, we are resilient and we have unwavering belief.

Not everyone has that.

RG: How can a new business get clientele?

JS: I truly believe it's all about building attention.

When you have the attention of people and they are aware and believe in what you and your business are all about, it's so much easier to transform that relationship from "audience" into "customer".

The part I think people get hung up on is they want that to happen overnight, and it doesn't work like that.

True relationships take time to build and you've got to be in it for the long haul if you truly want to create a sustainable business.

RG: What is an amazing moment your business gave you?

JS: It's not just one moment, but my favourite part of what Josh and I are building is that we get to do it together.

We're building our dream, side by side and I wouldn't give that up for the world.

RG: This book covers methods that people use to be successful. You guys embodied Immersion and Creation, by jumping in and immediately creating a unique product design, but I feel that your peer to peer networking is where you guys shined. Would you agree?

JS: Building a hyper-engaged community has truly changed the game for us and The Screw.

The Next Level: SUPERCHARGED

It's given us a way to get to know our audience on an extremely deep level, it allows us to take the pulse of what the community wants and it gives us the insight to ONLY create the products, content and live events that they actually want.

It's been huge and I cannot rave enough about what happens when you truly build a community of people all unified by a particular belief and rallying behind your brand.

I mean, it's pure magic.

RG: I feel like an entrepreneurial road map could be created that looks like this: Planning-Gathering-Creating-Launching-Selling-Assessing-Social Self Promotion-Adjusting-Improving. Would you agree or would you alter it?

JS: I would approach it differently, to be honest.

Here's how I would do it now if I had to start all over again.

- Create a community (FB group)
- Participate and give it your all
- Start taking notice of what different pain points/interest areas/questions people discuss in the group
- Compile a list of those
- Poll the community to find out the interest areas they are most interested in
- Create that
- Offer it to the community
- Tweak and make adjustments
- Create your sales funnel
- Market and promote it outside of the community
- Continue to tweak and improve

The Next Level: SUPERCHARGED

RG: If a person walked up to you and offered you $5000 for your best three pieces of advice for new business owners, what would that advice be?

JS: Just $5,000? Ha ha ha! I kid, I kid.

They would be:

- Create a community of people and talk TO them, not AT them
- Get clear on what your core offer is going to be and build a sales funnel around that
- Hang in there because it's going to be hard and you're going to doubt yourself, but if you can just stick it out, it will pay off

The Next Level: SUPERCHARGED

Epilogue

In parting, I hope you have enjoyed this book. I had a great time researching various methods of skill and career building, creating the GMOSC so people can rate their skills, and interviewing five amazing people that have made an impact in their chosen skills.

In your quest for rapid advancement, remember a few fundamentals:

*Society views formal education as the most "legitimate" way to become intelligent. This is a common misconception

*Intelligence can be spread across several fields, aptitudes, and practices. You may do poorly in one career and be on the cover of a magazine for another

*You will show the fastest growth by pursuing a career or skill in something that REALLY interests you.

The Next Level: SUPERCHARGED

Learning Worksheets

The following worksheets are designed to help you use Next Level concepts to maximize your learning. Here is how they work. Fill in the desired skill you want to improve in. Look up the GMOSC and give yourself an honest assessment of your skill level.

Choose 2-4 Next Level techniques that are best suited for your goal (BIG HINT: Use the "Most Likely Practitioners" as a guide).

I have given you four examples at the bottom to show you best practices in four different skills. Not all techniques work with all skills, but if you choose the right ones, you will have AMAZING results. Here are a few guidelines:

*languages, athletics and musical instruments both require hours of practice so Repetition is a good choice

*any goal that is education or creative based can be greatly aided by Neutropics

*anything that is complex/technical can use Diagramming to great results

*anything related to business branding or business growth needs Creation

The Next Level: SUPERCHARGED

What do I want to become brilliant at?

Where am I on the GMOSC at it?

What 2-4 Next Level techniques are best suited for learning this skill/job?

1. 2.

3. 4.

EXAMPLES:

Sports/Athletics:
Repetition/Emulation
Immersion/HLSME

Language:
Repetition/Diagramming
Tutelage/Research/Trifecta

Writing:
Creation/Immersion
Research/Tutelage
Neutropic Drugs

Business Growth:
Diagramming/Trifecta
HLSME/Emulation
Mastermind/Groups

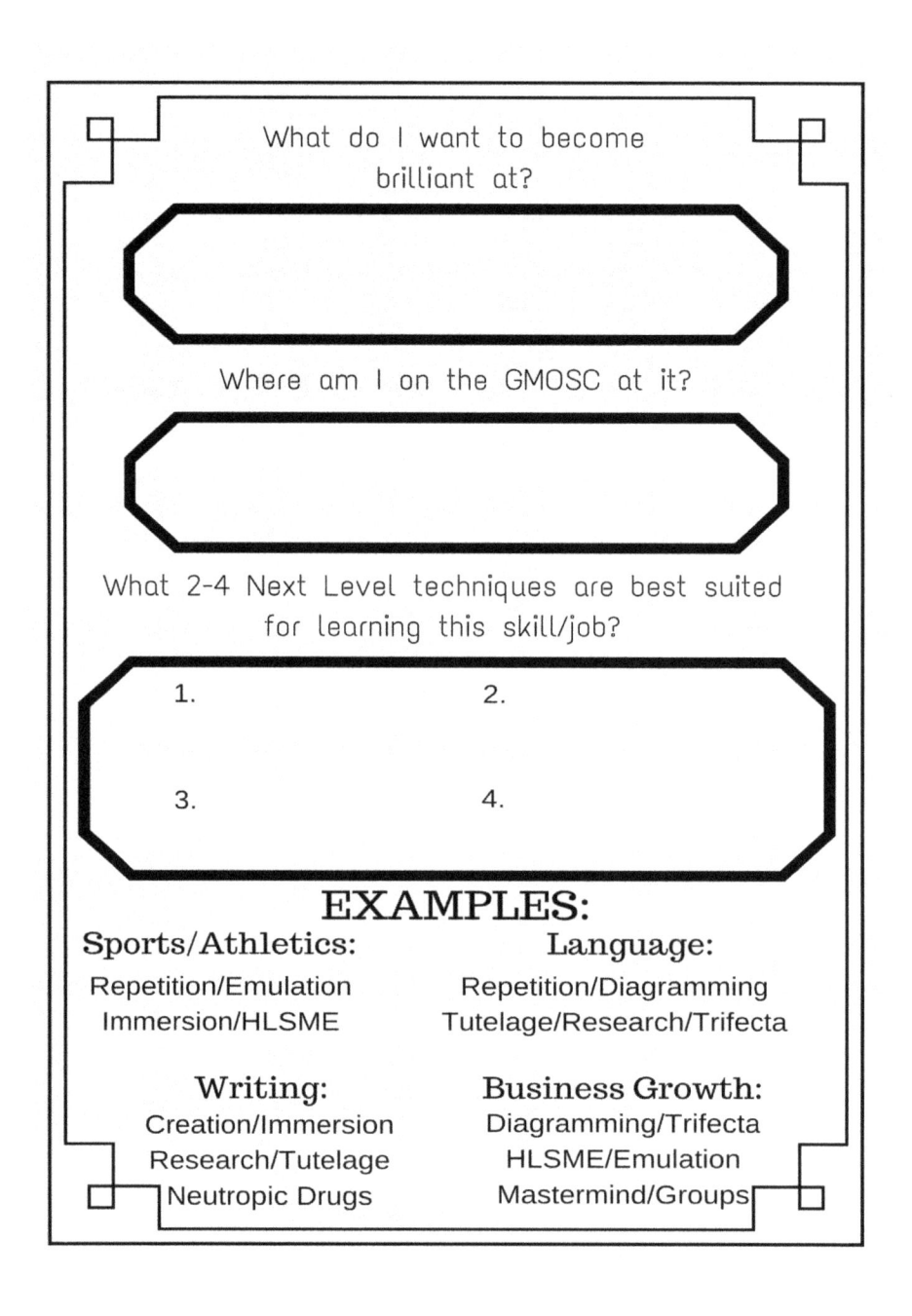

The Next Level: SUPERCHARGED

What do I want to become brilliant at?

Where am I on the GMOSC at it?

What 2-4 Next Level techniques are best suited for learning this skill/job?

1.
2.
3.
4.

EXAMPLES:

Sports/Athletics:
Repetition/Emulation
Immersion/HLSME

Language:
Repetition/Diagramming
Tutelage/Research/Trifecta

Writing:
Creation/Immersion
Research/Tutelage
Neutropic Drugs

Business Growth:
Diagramming/Trifecta
HLSME/Emulation
Mastermind/Groups

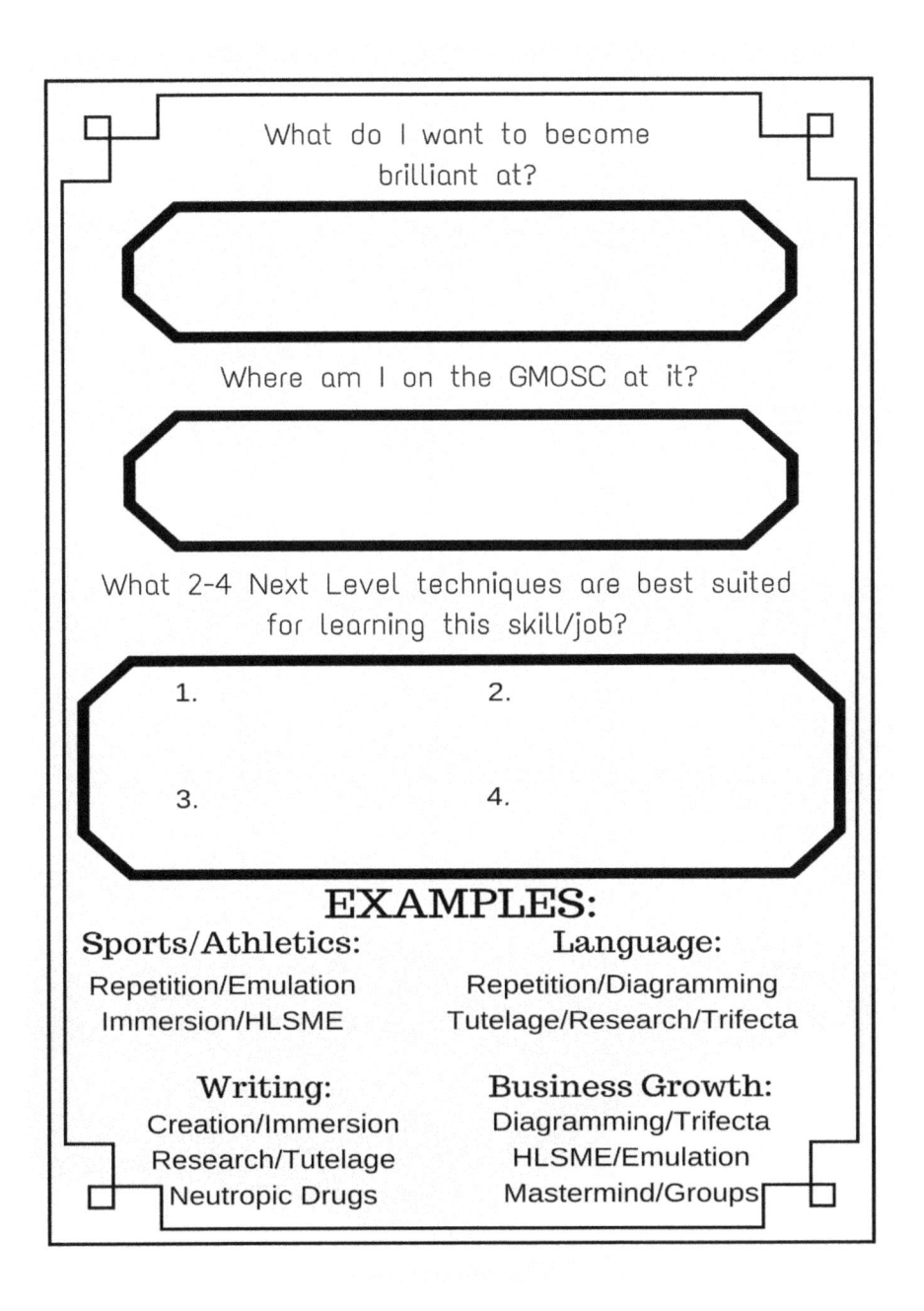

The Next Level: SUPERCHARGED

What do I want to become brilliant at?

Where am I on the GMOSC at it?

What 2-4 Next Level techniques are best suited for learning this skill/job?

1. 2.

3. 4.

EXAMPLES:

Sports/Athletics:
Repetition/Emulation
Immersion/HLSME

Language:
Repetition/Diagramming
Tutelage/Research/Trifecta

Writing:
Creation/Immersion
Research/Tutelage
Neutropic Drugs

Business Growth:
Diagramming/Trifecta
HLSME/Emulation
Mastermind/Groups

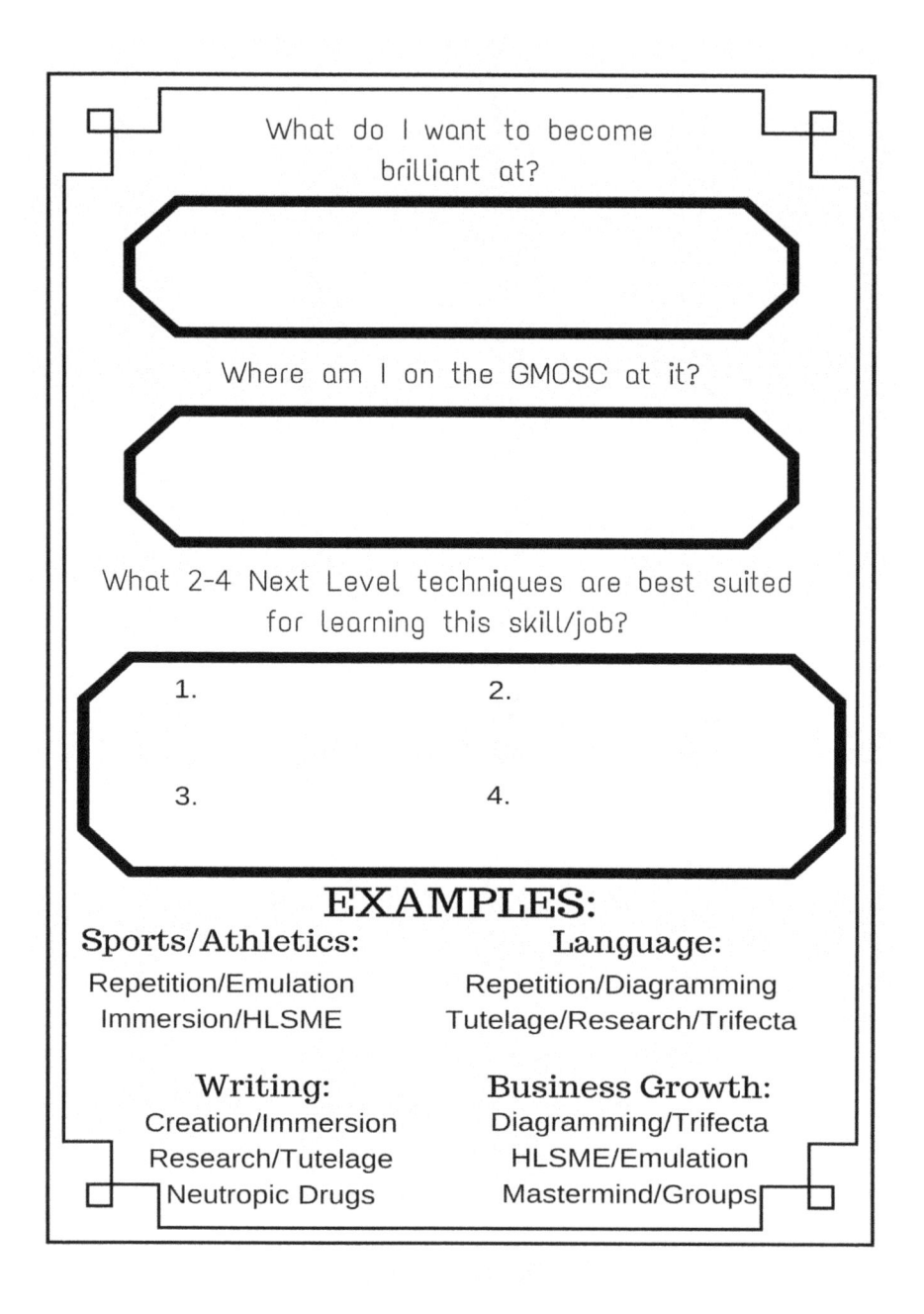

The Next Level: SUPERCHARGED

What do I want to become brilliant at?

Where am I on the GMOSC at it?

What 2-4 Next Level techniques are best suited for learning this skill/job?

1.　　　　　　　2.

3.　　　　　　　4.

EXAMPLES:

Sports/Athletics:
Repetition/Emulation
Immersion/HLSME

Language:
Repetition/Diagramming
Tutelage/Research/Trifecta

Writing:
Creation/Immersion
Research/Tutelage
Neutropic Drugs

Business Growth:
Diagramming/Trifecta
HLSME/Emulation
Mastermind/Groups

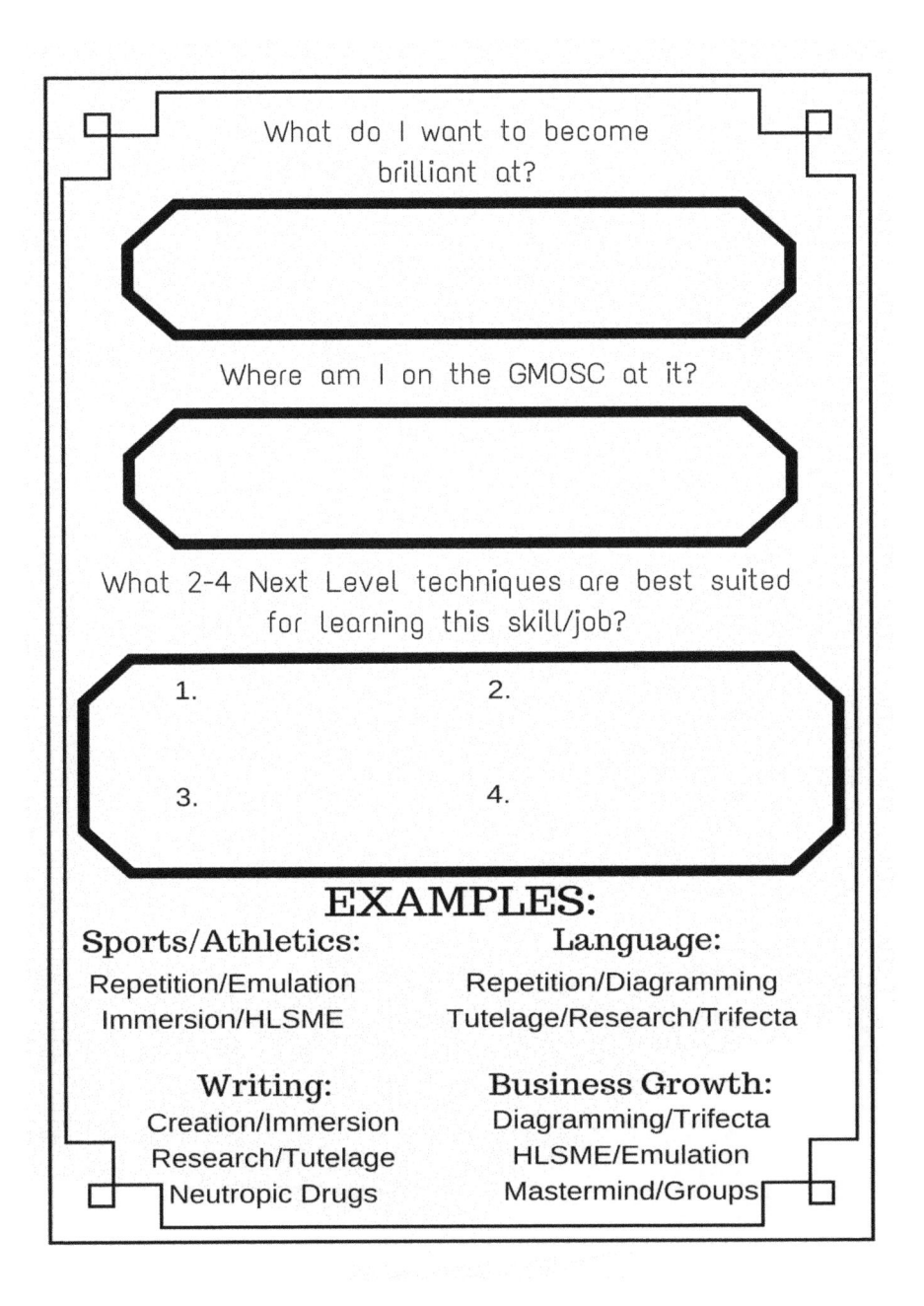

The Next Level: SUPERCHARGED

What do I want to become brilliant at?

Where am I on the GMOSC at it?

What 2-4 Next Level techniques are best suited for learning this skill/job?

1.　　　　　2.

3.　　　　　4.

EXAMPLES:

Sports/Athletics:
Repetition/Emulation
Immersion/HLSME

Language:
Repetition/Diagramming
Tutelage/Research/Trifecta

Writing:
Creation/Immersion
Research/Tutelage
Neutropic Drugs

Business Growth:
Diagramming/Trifecta
HLSME/Emulation
Mastermind/Groups

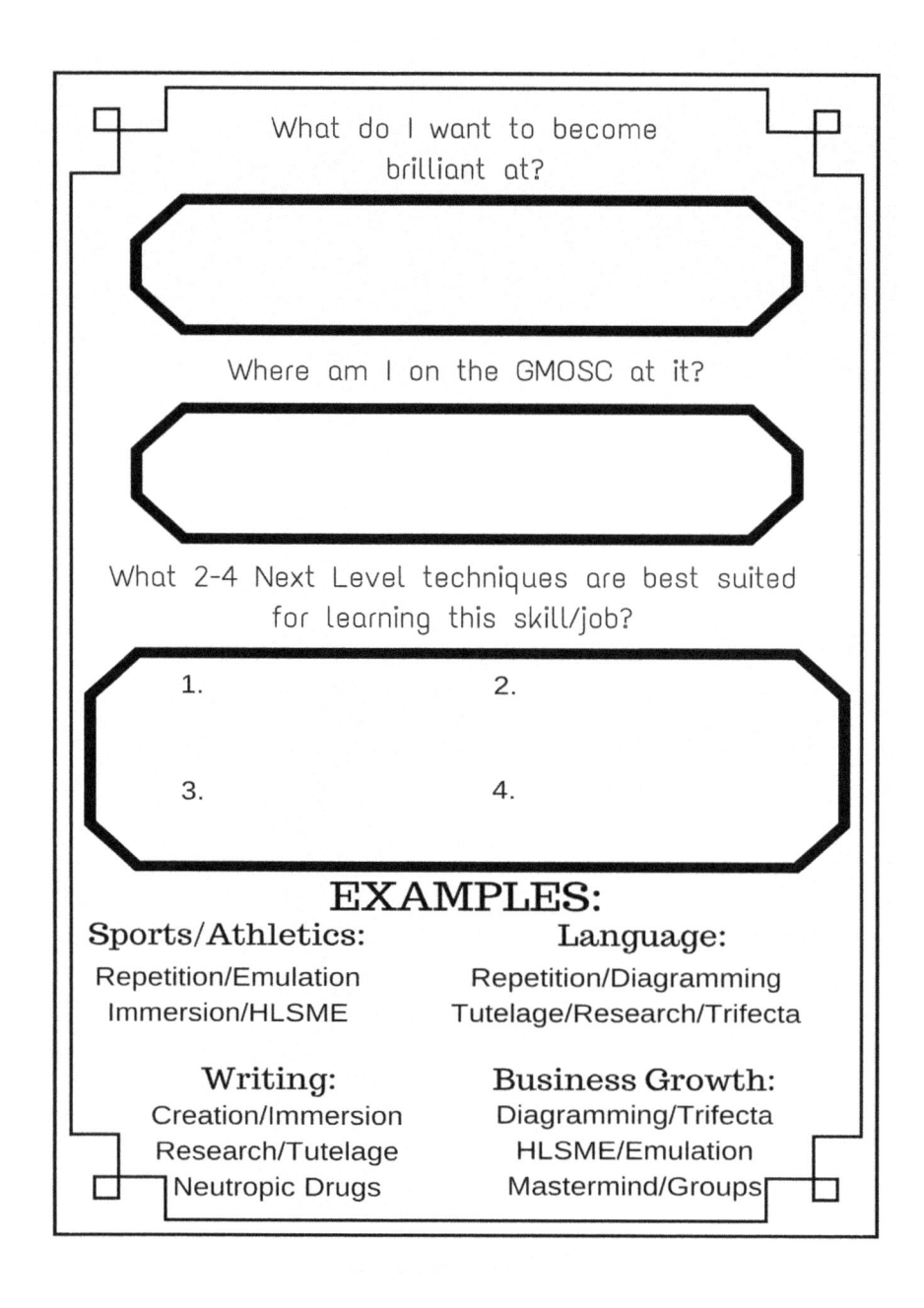

The Next Level: SUPERCHARGED

Author Bio

Dr. Rob Garcia is the founder of SHIFT Magazine, a Technical Sergeant in the Air Force Reserve, author of seven books and CEO of Blue Dragon Enterprises. He enjoys beach runs, cooking Italian cuisine, skateboarding, and working with low income teens.
He can be reached at dragonsgold76@gmail.com.

The Next Level: SUPERCHARGED

Got a Next Level success story? Did this book help you accomplish or learn something amazing? I would LOVE to hear about it and possibly feature it in a future book or my magazine, SHIFT.

Email all stories to dragonsgold76@gmail.com

Dr. Rob